Potty Training Sucks

What to Do When
Diapers Make You Miserable

Joanne Kimes
with Kathleen Laccinole

Technical review by Linda Sonna, Ph.D.

Adams Media
Avon, Massachusetts

Published by
Adams Media, an F+W Publications Company
57 Littlefield Street, Avon, MA 02322 U.S.A.
www.adamsmedia.com

ISBN 10: 1-59337-630-8
ISBN 13: 978-1-59337-630-7
Printed in the United States of America.

J I H G F E D C B A

Library of Congress Cataloging-in-Publication Data
Kimes, Joanne.
Potty training sucks / Joanne Kimes with Kathleen Laccinole ;
technical review by Linda Sonna.
p. cm.
ISBN-13: 978-1-59337-630-7 (pbk.)
ISBN-10: 1-59337-630-8 (pbk.)
1. Toilet training. 2. Toilet training—Humor.
I. Laccinole, Kathleen. II. Sonna, Linda. III. Title.
HQ770.5.K55 2007
649'.62—dc22
2007002035

This publication is designed to provide accurate and authoritative information with regard to the subject matter covered. It is sold with the understanding that the publisher is not engaged in rendering professional medical advice. If assistance is required, the services of a competent medical professional should be sought. The views expressed are solely those of the author.

— From a *Declaration of Principles* jointly adopted by a Committee of the American Bar Association and a Committee of Publishers and Associations

Many of the designations used by manufacturers and sellers to distinguish their product are claimed as trademarks. Where those designations appear in this book and Adams Media was aware of a trademark claim, the designations have been printed with initial capital letters.

This book is available at quantity
discounts for bulk purchases.
For information, please call
1-800-289-0963.

*To my mother, Micki Fink, who did a great job
teaching me how to use the potty . . . and
everything else I needed to know in life.
I love you!
–Joanne*

*To Greta and William,
my favorite number one and number two.
– Kathleen*

contents

Acknowledgments ix

Chapter 1
The Poop on Potty Training 1
Under Pressure 3
When to Begin the Process of Elimination. 7
To Everything There Is a Season. 11
How Long Will This Be Going On? 14
To Insanity and Beyond 18
Potty Paraphernalia 24
Potty Mouth 31

Chapter 2
Let's Get This Potty Started! 37
Potty Training in the Fantasy World 40
Incentives, Bribes, and the Dreaded C-Word 44
New Age Craze-Y 49

What Your Mother-in-Law Doesn't Know 53
The Dr. Phil Method 55
The "Make Someone Else Do It" Method 60
The "Do Nothing" Method 68

Chapter 3
Urine for Some Fun Now! **71**
Connecting the Urge with the Purge 72
The Trouble with Boys 76
My Girl Wants to Potty All the Time 81
Holding It In 85
Potty Proclivities 93
Don't Get Pissed Off .97

Chapter 4
The Scoop on Poop **105**
The Poop Hold 108
Much Ado about Poo (a.k.a. Constipation) 116
Wipe Out 122
Potty Poopers 128
Heinie Hygiene 131

Chapter 5
Accidents Happen . . . Again and Again
and Again **135**
The Anatomy of a Mishap 139
Plan B 144
An Ounce of Prevention Is Worth
    a Pound of Poop 149
Jump on the Night Train 155

Chapter 6
Be Careful What You Whiz For 161
Stress. 164
Public Toilets: The Chamber of Horrors
    for the Germ-Phobic Mom 167
Wine, as with Potty Training, Improves
    with Age 173
Bodily Malfunctions 176
From Potty to Porcelain. 181
My Toilet Runneth Over 184
Till Death or Doo-Doo You Part 190

Chapter 7
Congratulations! 197

Appendix: Resources Section 201

Index 209

acknowledgments

First and foremost, I'd like to thank my daughter, Emily, for being such a pain in the ass to potty train that she supplied me lots of great material for this book.

A big thank you to my co-writer, Kathleen Laccinole, who is not only an incredibly talented writer, but has a great potty mouth as well.

Thanks to Gary Krebs at Adams Media for believing in the Sucks Series and making it possible for me to have the best stay-at-home career possible!

To Jennifer Kushnier and Meredith O'Hayre, my wonderful editors at Adams, for bumping this book up a notch and smoothing out all of its crinkles.

And of course, I'm forever grateful to my wonderful husband, Jeff, for being the kind of father who rolled up his sleeves, plugged up his nose, and changed lots of dirty diapers. I love you!

Chapter 1

the poop on potty training

You are about to enter another dimension. A dimension of both sight and sound, of unlimited Pull-Ups, potty books, and power struggles. A dimension where time and space have no meaning, and reason does not exist. You've made it through the birthing, the nursing, the endless sleepless nights, the teething, the weaning, and all the in-betweening. You've survived food fights in five-star restaurants, crayon drawing on newly painted walls, and all-out refusal to wear anything but a faded princess outfit or a too-tight Superman costume. And while you thought these dimensions were difficult to bear, the truth is that they pale in comparison to what lies ahead. So hang on tight, sister, for the next stop is—the Potty Zone!

Just when you thought you had this whole parenting thing handled, you realize that a whole new exhausting adventure awaits you. Around every corner there are new videos to buy, new stains to pretreat, and new cleansers to buy that will remove excrement from your beautiful new rug. Your college-educated, once-articulate vocabulary will now consist of phrases like "Do you wanna make tinkle?" and "Is it poopie time?"

As frustrating as the potty-training phase may be, I promise that there will be an end. There will be a light at the end of this stinky, messy, smelly tunnel, and you will get through it. One day your shopping cart will be free of bulk-size containers of Huggies, half-ton boxes of diaper wipes, and gallon jugs of Desitin. No more pee-stained pants, poo-stained car seats, or Diaper Genie cartridges to wrangle. And no more physical therapy from having to lug around that oversized, back-straining diaper bag that weighs more than your big-boned Aunt Martha does after eating Thanksgiving dinner.

Yes, I know it's dark now. Dare I say, dark as poo. But fear not, my friend. The Potty Zone is a mere pit stop in parenting. And after your toddler learns to excuse himself, go to the bathroom, and wipe himself so clean that his rear end sparkles without any assistance from you, it may just bring a tear to your eye. Believe it or not, after all the potty training is behind you, you might actually miss the days of the midnight diaper changes, pee fountains, and explosive poops. Ha! Just kidding! The truth is that the day that your child is successfully potty trained will be as memorable as your wedding day, the birth of your babies, and the final episode of *Sex and the City* when you find out Mr. Big's real name. So pull up a potty chair, and let's get down to business.

NOTE: This book contains an endless amount of shameless puns that I couldn't stop myself from writing, but I did try to keep them down to a wee-wee minimum . . . shoot! There I go again!

Under Pressure

Before I reproduced, I had always viewed the state of motherhood as an awe-inspiring, almost secret society that I was not a member. And with every egg that dropped each month into my fertile, yet unfarmed womb, I longed to belong. I would push my face up against the proverbial glass wall that separated me from all the mutual maternal experiences: the pregnancy stories, the birthing nightmares, the baby pictures, the nursing anecdotes, and the shared glances of understanding between all mothers in this clan. It was as if parenting a baby was an invisible link on a chain that bound women together in a sisterhood of mommies, and I wanted desperately to be a charm on that bracelet of life.

Then, after years of painful dating struggles and brief thoughts of throwing in the towel and becoming a lesbian, I finally found myself a farmer with good fertile seed. After months of infertility and charting my cycle with the accuracy of a NASA launch, I finally got a membership key, otherwise known as a baby, that would unlock the door to this sacred club. Yes, I was finally a mom! But it didn't take long to realize that motherhood is not a club at all. To the contrary, motherhood is a cutthroat competition between overtired and overstressed females in which only the strong survive. When Darwin developed his theory of survival of the fittest, he must have been studying only the mommy finches. I soon discovered

that all the warm, fuzzy camaraderie I was cov-
eting was, in fact, just a tactic in the mommy
game. I immediately learned that motherhood is
really about who can do the most, the best, and
the fastest.

By now, if you're like most of us procreating
women, you've realized that being a mommy is
an exercise in failure, and that you always feel
like you're losing in some aspect of your life.
If you've got your kids on track, then you're
neglecting your career. If you spend more time
at the office, then your husband feels neglected.
If you pay more attention to your husband, then
you feel like your kids are losing out. It's a vicious
cycle that has spun its little wheels ever since the
invention of motherhood.

If you have the time and strength to do extra-
credit mommy work, like attend a weekly Gymboree class, you're one-upped by the woman across
the street who has her kid enrolled in Gymboree
and karate—plus makes her own baby food, hand
knits all of her kid's clothes, and is teaching little
Tallulah both French and Japanese.

But now you're entering the Big Kahuna
of all competitions—potty training. Well,
my friend, be prepared, for there is no greater
imaginary gauge to good parenting than getting

your kid to use the toilet. Generally, the starting gun to this competition is fired off about your kid's second birthday (even earlier if your mother-in-law tells you that her kids were all potty trained by one). It's about this time when one of your mommy friends brags that her kid used the potty for the first time last night, you notice that some of the kids in your playgroup have stopped wearing diapers, and your damn neighbor shows you that she's throwing baby Tallulah's potty chair in the trash because it's no longer needed.

Okay, let me set you straight. Your mother-in-law is senile; half the kids in your play group have diapers on under their underwear (and their moms are sweating bullets worrying they're going to be found out); and the woman across the street is either a big fat liar or a robot her husband bought from a mail-order catalogue.

The point to all this is that there's no winning the mommy game, so do yourself a favor and don't even play it. Don't give into external pressures to wean your baby, get him to sleep by a certain time or through the night, or sign him up for Mensa just because you think that's what you should be doing. And don't even consider potty training until you and your little one are good and ready. If your "friends" or family are making you feel pressured about any aspect of your mothering, then avoid them for the time being. There are plenty of us out there who think you are doing everything just perfectly.

Most importantly, don't put pressure on yourself. Many mommies are their own worst enemies, and frankly, right now you need all the support you can get. Doesn't it seem like just yesterday when your little guy was the last of his peers to walk, and now he's constantly trying to run into the street? And how you once thought your little Petunia would never talk, and now you can't get her to stop screaming, "I want that!" in every store at the mall? If you have a toddler, you already have enough legitimate things to stress over without inventing nonexistent deadlines and dilemmas. So take a deep breath, go easy on yourself, and for heaven's sake, drop little Petunia off at Grandma's whenever you go to the mall. It'll save you a fortune in "treasures"!

When to Begin the Process of Elimination

So when is it time to get your behind in gear and get your kid's behind on a potty? It's when your child is ready, willing, and able, and not one minute sooner, no matter how much you really, really want it to be. Like walking and talking, toileting is a developmental phase, not the least bit indicative of intelligence or physical prowess. It will happen in "doo" time. If you delve into the process before your baby wants to and is able to be potty trained, then you're setting yourself up for failure—or at least an awfully big struggle that involves a heck of a lot of screaming and crying (mostly yours). And you and Junior don't need conflict so early on in your relationship. Heck, you've only been together for a couple of years. You're still in the honeymoon phase, so let's not blow it. There's plenty of time for pain and suffering down the road, when your son wants to quit high school to pursue his dream of becoming a professional skateboarder and your daughter brings home her new boyfriend, Fang.

It's true, we've all heard about the phantom baby who was potty trained at eleven months. And don't forget about that four-year-old who's still sporting extra-large Pampers Supreme. Truth be told, the perfectly average baby generally trains somewhere in between. If you want to know if your little offspring is ready, ask yourself whether you've seen any of these tell-tale signs that he's ready to step up to the plate . . . or in this case, the potty:

1. Is your child physically ready? Is he able to stay dry for at least two hours at a stretch during the day, and does he often wake up dry after naps?
2. Does your child have predictable, regular BMs? (You may have figured out his schedule accidentally, like when his regular 5:00 bath had to be moved to 6:00 so you wouldn't keep asking yourself, "Why the heck does my kid keep pooping in the bath?")
3. Can you tell when your child's about to go the bathroom? He might pause for a moment, make a face, or perhaps even hide.
4. Is your child able to listen to or follow simple instructions? It helps when you are trying to explain that the pee-pee goes inside the toilet, not around the toilet.
5. Does your child dislike wearing dirty diapers? This is a tough one, as the ingenious invention of disposable diapers has made uncomfortable, soiled nappies a thing of the past. The commercials tout their

comfort as the number-one reason to buy them—and we do what they ask, by the truckload. In the olden days, babies were miserable when wet or dirty. Now, they hardly even notice. Therefore, I believe that disposable diapers have caused the entire human race to delay potty training for pure convenience sake. Still, a wet, albeit disposable diaper can't possibly be as comfortable as a nice, dry pair of good old cotton undies.

6. Speaking of which, does your child show a desire to wear big-kid underpants sporting pictures of princesses or Ninja Turtles? And while we're at it, how does he feel about the toilet or the potty chair? Has he been looking at it? Has he climbed aboard for a trial run? Interest is key when dealing with toddlers.

7. Can your child pull down his pants and pull them back up again? As you can guess, this handy dandy trick would be helpful in mastering the art of going to the bathroom.

8. Does your child like to watch you use the bathroom? I know it feels strange to have someone examining you at one of your

most intimate moments, but Junior is just studying up. When Junior wants to mimic you using the toilet, he's ready to learn. And when Junior wants to mimic his friends using the toilet, you're home free.

9. Most importantly, is your child starting a preschool in the fall that requires him to be potty trained? (Okay, technically I know it's not a sign, but still . . .)

To Everything There Is a Season

As with most things in life, when it comes to potty training, timing is everything. Now that you've determined that your little tax deduction is ready to be toilet trained, we can only hope that all the planets are aligned as well. As you probably know well by now, toddlers do not like change. If you're going to pull a head trip as huge as making your kid give up his diaper, then everything else in his life is going to have to remain absolutely perfect.

Before you pull out that potty chair and change your baby's life forever, make sure there are no other tidal waves of trauma on the horizon. A new baby, a move, a new day care, a new cable provider—anything that would ripple the still waters of your baby's simple world will definitely frustrate the process of potty training, if not obliterate it completely. If you're planning on moving next week, postpone your potty-training plans until after you have settled in the new house. For the love of Elmo, if you're about to take that family trip to Mount Rushmore, wait until you return home to potty train your child— unless, that is, you enjoy misery in a ridiculously crowded tourist attraction.

In addition to choosing a calm time to potty train, you also have to choose a calm season. Ideally, summer is the best season to potty train your child (unless you live in California, Hawaii, or Southern France—the potty-training capitals of the world, where the climate allows for year-round training). When the weather is warm, your little love muffin can run around the house in the buff, or at least scantily clad, which makes the "tossing of the little one onto the potty when he starts to poop" quite easy. You can even put your little love muffin and the potty chair outside and let him have his own mini nudist colony. If he has an accident, then you just hose him down like a fighting dog and get on with your day.

“ My daughter peed in the back yard all the time and it made little dead patches all over the grass. I knew it'd cost a lot of money to have a kid, but I wasn't counting on extras like resodding after our kid was potty trained.”

—Emily

NOTE: If you live in Arizona or any other desert community, leaving your kid outside, naked, in 115-degree heat is not such a good idea.

If you live in a place with four distinct seasons, consider yourself unlucky. Not only does the winter bring you special challenges, like shoveling your driveway and walking on icy sidewalks, it also brings special challenges in potty training your kid. For there are not many things worse than hearing your kid say, "I gotta go *now*!" when he's wearing eighteen layers of clothing including bib overalls with the stuck clasp that you never can seem to undo when your fingers are frozen. Don't get me wrong. I don't think you should postpone potty training due to cold weather. That's just plain silly. But on the other hand, if your kid is not ready to train during the freezing snows of winter, then great. If he's starting to show signs during that blizzard, well . . . you

can wait a little, can't you? On the other hand, if
he's passed his "signs" test with flying colors, and
is ready to train, then train you must. As with
everything in your career as a mother, you will
somehow adapt.

When this happens, turn up your thermo-
stat, take off the layers, and go for it. Just make
sure that you stick with easy-access elastic waistbands and snaps, and avoid tricky buttons, zip-
pers, hooks, and most of all, those gosh-forsaken
bib overalls! Though it's cold outside, there'll
be warm pee-pee a-flowin' inside. Then again,
if potty training during winter doesn't appeal
to you at all, you can always move to California,
Hawaii, or my choice, Southern France.

How Long Will This Be Going On?

It's the question of the ages. Along with "Is there
life on other planets?" and "Who let the dog
out . . . who, who, who, who, who?" millions of
parents each day ask desperately, "How long is
it going to take to get my kid out of diapers?"
I'm sorry, my distraught friend, but there is no
absolute answer to this question. Potty training
is a process, and it varies from kid to kid because,

unfortunately, every child is different. Sad but true. I know that right now this is a bitter pill to swallow, but trust me, this difference isn't always a bad thing. One day, when you look at some of your child's classmates and cringe at their oddness and all-out bad behavior, this will make you happy. You'll thank your lucky stars that even though your child took two years to potty train, at least he doesn't bring in his booger collection for show-and-tell.

I know we've all heard stories of the child who was trained in one day. But we've also heard stories of babies who slept through the night straight out of the chute and of women who were actually horny during pregnancy. Personally, I think these are all urban legends, and should be written off along with Richard Gere's infamous gerbil incident.

Nevertheless, I won't lie. Potty training could take a little time. It's yet another one of the proverbial "baby steps" scenarios that requires patience, patience, and even more patience. Try to recall, if you will, when you were teaching your little one to feed himself. First it was the "squeeze the food through the hands" phase. Then it was the "throw the food all over Mommy phase." Next came the "drop the food on the floor phase" and then finally—TA DA!—the "hold the food on a spoon" phase. The heavens parted and a chorus of angels burst into song! But only for a moment, for soon, that spoon was used as an instrument to fling the food across the room. Oh, well. Rome wasn't built in a day, and it will probably take even longer to potty train your child.

Personally, I don't believe this question speaks to time so much as it does to definition. How long it takes to potty train your child depends on what you consider a potty-trained child to be. An overly competitive mother might throw her baby onto the pot at the exact moment a poop is coming out, catch the poop in the pot like some sort of celebrated outfielder, and then claim the "my baby is potty trained" prize. To other mothers, "potty trained" might mean their child is able to pee on the potty, and not around it. Never mind that the very same child needs to do her number twos in a diaper until she's eight years old. Other moms consider peeing and pooping in the potty to be the two necessary components in the "potty trained" declaration. These are the same people who never cheat on their taxes and always pay their bills on time. Still others count night dryness in the "potty trained" formula as well. These are the people who . . . well, I have no idea who these people are. If the kid is peeing and pooping in the potty, give him some credit.

And what about the variations? What about the kids who are potty trained at home, but then can only use the bathroom at home? Or the kids who will only use the potty chair, so you have to tote the darned thing with you everywhere you go? Are they technically potty trained? Or what about the kid who pees in the potty for five days, then stops? Is he potty trained? Semi-trained? Half-decaf trained, with an extra shot of espresso?

You see, it's all how you look at it. Your kid is potty trained when you say he is. The rest is all semantics. And if you're psyching yourself out worrying about "how long," and "what qualifies as," then just say he's potty trained, even though he isn't, and be done with it. That way the

66 There's this mom in our playgroup who constantly brags about how her son is fully potty trained and has yet to have one accident even though he's not even two years old. The other moms and I constantly offer him juice boxes when he's on our watch just to see if we can get him to pee in his pants! 99

—Robin

pressure will be gone. After all, he did pee in the dog bowl just the other day. And in my book, that's potty trained.

To Insanity and Beyond

Before you begin the process of housebreaking your child, you must get in the right mindset. This would be one of "no expectations," and "if it happens it happens" kinds of mindsets. In other words, the goal would be to feel Zen with a capital "Z." Unfortunately, in real life, most real mommies only feel Angry with a capital "A." In an ideal world full of rainbows and calorie-free desserts, a parent wouldn't get upset over resistance, aggravation, or accidents. In fact, most all the books you'll read about potty training tell you that any big reaction from you will only make the situation worse. Personally, I'd like to invite the authors of these fantasy books to come over to my house and clean up the "Close Encounters of the Third Kind" sculpture that my child just constructed out of the contents of her diaper.

Let's face it: We grownups are only human. We're tired, overworked, and underappreciated, and sometimes it's just plain impossible to remain calm in the face of unrelenting challenges. Especially if those challenges stink, stain, and are a big freaking drag to clean up. So don't beat yourself up too badly if you react to the stresses of potty training. On that same note, however, do your double-fudge best to keep those emotions in check. Take a deep breath, count to ten, or have an apple martini—whatever works for you to keep the blood pressure in the black. And realize going in that there will be times when you're frustrated to the nth degree. You can tell your kid what to eat, what to wear, and what time to go to bed, but the one thing you can't do is *make* him go to the bathroom in the toilet. You are only the guide, the teacher, and the mentor. As soon as you realize that you can't control the way he excretes, the more in control you'll actually feel. Remember, you can lead a horse to water, but you cannot make him drink it and then take a leak in the potty.

The bottom line is that only Junior can control his bottom, and believe me, Junior is keenly aware of this fact. In fact, you can rest assured that he's going to work it, and work it like only a toddler can. He's going to have you do everything you swore you'd never do before you went into this potty-training venture, from giving him candy to letting him watch all the TV he wants to bribing him with cold hard cash. You'll ply him with forbidden, sugar-ridden, soda in a futile attempt to produce more urine and ergo more practice time. And when that doesn't work, you'll sit on the cold bathroom floor for hours on end while he regales you with cute, aimless stories and adorable faces, knowing full well that he's not going to make nothin' in that pot, but loving your complete and total attention in the meantime.

And when you and your husband start fighting about the fact that you haven't left the house in twenty-two days because you don't want to abandon the "process," then the little pisser knows he has you over a barrel. For heaven's sake, stop! If you're not careful, potty training can take over your life. It will seep into the cracks of your world and explode it from the inside out. Don't let this happen. Put your trust in Mother Nature. Your child will be potty trained, most likely sometime after she can find her belly button and before she sneaks her first cigarette. Somehow, some way, it will happen, even if you do absolutely nothing. I promise.

Yes, I know you're afraid. You're very, very, afraid. What if you're doing it all wrong? What if your baby ends up emotionally scarred?

Pu-leez! Have you ever heard of anyone who suffered from post–potty-training stress disorder?" Have you ever seen a talk show about it? An article in *Time* magazine? No. That's because it does not exist. At least it doesn't exist for the toddler. Now mommies, on the other hand, well mommies certainly go through some stresses, but the kid seems to go through this stage quite well. That's because toddlers don't have much of a long-term memory for things like this. When they get older, they don't even remember potty training—or, for that matter, the time you "accidentally" pushed them off the swing when they kept yelling "Harder, Mommy!!" over and over and over again.

If you feel like you're ready for the games to begin and Junior is primed and up for the challenge—and if you have the extra-strength fortitude, and extra-strength aspirin—just keep to the following top ten list of potty-training doo-doos and don'ts to keep your attitude, and your little one's cooperation, on the potty train track:

Top Ten Potty-Training Doo-Doos and Don'ts

1. Doo be positive and upbeat about potty training. Get Junior excited about the

process. Look at some books and videos. Sing some songs. Woo hoo!

2. Doo practice, practice, practice. Allow Junior to explore his potty seat or toilet before you begin. Let him live with the idea, and the potty chair, for a few days, maybe even take some dry runs.

3. Don't force your child to sit on the potty. We all know how well forcing works with toddlers. And nagging ain't gonna get you much further.

4. Don't make a big deal of failures or successes. Otherwise, you'll be turning over the keys to your life to an unreasonable three-year-old.

5. Don't lament your child's "growing up." You want Junior to want to be a big boy, not dread it.

6. Don't be grossed out. If you start to gag every time you have to clean up a misplaced dump off the area rug, Junior might like it and want you to do it again and again and again.

7. Don't mess with Mother Nature. Do not give your child laxatives, enemas, or any other TV-movie-of-the-week torture treatment unless recommended by your pediatrician.

8. Doo encourage independence without setting Junior up for failure. Let him use the potty in private, pull down his pants, or even wipe a pee-pee all by himself, but don't expect him to master the whole big-time operation from the get go—unless, of course, you like poop on every conceivable surface of your bathroom.

9. Doo keep a good supply of cleaning products at hand. The only thing worse than an accident is a kid playing in the accident while you're madly hunting for the disinfectant spray.

10. And finally, doo remember to stock your freezer with the fixings for those apple martinis. They really are quite yummy!

So lighten up, sweetie. Stop worrying, and above all keep your sense of humor. My friend Maxine once told me that potty training your kid is a lot like dieting. If you step on the scale and you've lost just one pound, then your whole day is fantastic. Likewise, if Junior gets his tinkle inside the toilet one time, you're walking on air. So here's wishing you long life, health, happiness . . . and few tinkles in the toilet.

Potty Paraphernalia

Who'd have thought that something as basic and natural as answering the call of nature would require so much manmade crap? It's bad enough that you'll be paying off baby furniture well into the college years. Now you've got to take out a second mortgage on your home in order to finance potty training as well. Okay, so maybe I exaggerate a little (you should pay off your baby furniture by middle school), but still, there's a lot of stuff being marketed to the worn-weary new parent. And while you could probably get by with just a simple hole in the backyard, you might want to take into consideration some of the following items.

Potty Chair Versus Toilet

Oy vey, the stress of it! Decisions, decisions. While it probably seems insignificant to your average Joe, to the toddler parent, it might as well be Sophie's Choice.

The potty chair is a small portable bowl that comes encased in a box, sometimes with a lid. Take Junior shopping with you and let him pick out his own potty chair, as this will help stimulate his interest in what lies ahead. My daughter went for the standard white plastic model, which was sturdy, easy to clean, and, more importantly to her, easy to decorate. A package of stickers and some markers can go a long way in personalizing a potty chair (and a wall, if you're not careful!). Letting your child create his very own throne will only make him want to sit on it more.

The toilet—is, well . . . it's your toilet. If your child wants to go straight to the big time, you'll need a toilet-seat adapter. This is a circular gizmo that fits on top of your toilet and prevents the apple of your eye from slipping in and getting flushed out of your life. A good fit is key, as you don't want your toddler sliding off or getting pinched in his delicate nether-regions (which is likely to postpone potty training until puberty). If your child wants to start off on the toilet, it's a good idea to provide a sturdy footstool so he can actually climb up onto the potty or, if he shoots while standing, reach the bowl.

NOTE: If you are working with a boy, and he likes to sit while he tinkles, you'll want to stay away from the "spray deflector." It's a plastic lip that's attached to some potty seat adapters (and potty seats) that's supposed to prevent pee from shooting all over the place. These deflectors could make it impossible for your little guy to get on or off the pot without scraping his "little guy." You'll find that your husband is especially concerned about this issue. So just teach him how to point down. Trust me, you'll feel better, your husband will feel better, and your son's "little guy" will feel better.

Which brings us back to the greater issue: Which instrument should you choose, the potty chair or the toilet seat? Well, my friend, this is entirely up to you. Actually, it's up to your toddler, as he's the one we're trying to cajole here.

Potty chairs are good in theory. They're small, portable, and easily cleaned. But the drag is that they are small, portable, and easily cleaned. The small size means your child will outgrow his sooner rather than later, and then you'll need to retrain your kid to use the actual toilet. The portability means, technically, that you can put it anywhere—your TV room, the kitchen, or on the roof of the house. If your kid gets attached, you'll be toting that disgusting little box everywhere you go, since your little love muffin will refuse to use any other toilet or potty chair in the whole entire universe. While they are certainly easy to clean, clean you must—*every time your kid uses it.* And frankly, it can get kinda gross. You have to pour the contents of the chair into the big toilet, then rinse and spray and wipe, oh my! Cleaning a toilet is waaaaay easier than cleaning a potty chair.

My suggestion is to use all the means you can to get your kid to use the toilet instead of a potty chair. Try to get your child geared up and excited about going to the bathroom on a toilet. Make a big deal out of it, have him watch you, encrust it with diamonds if necessary. Give your kid a snazzy new step stool and have him climb aboard the big porcelain throne. You'll have a kid who can pee anywhere, less cleaning up to do, and a crapper encrusted with jewels. What more could a girl want?

Training Pants: Plastic Versus Cotton

It's the rivalry of the modern age, right up there with Leno versus Letterman, Coke versus Pepsi, and SUV versus hybrid, and this one, too, is rife with conflict and controversy. When using training pants, should you get the plastic, disposable kind, or the cotton kind that you have to wash yourself? As with all other controversies in life, everyone seems to have an opinion. So let me not give you mine (at least not yet). Instead, I'll simply pass along a few facts.

To begin with, you could certainly keep your kids in diapers until he's ready to wear big-kid

underwear. But if you've decided to use training
pants, there are some things to know. The upside
of using training pants is that, like the toilet,
they get your little one all geared up for growing
up. Just putting them on sends your toddler into
"I'm almost a teenager" mode. It also gives him
a sense of control. Training pants are easier for a
toddler to deal with than diapers, and having an
accident is not a traumatic or embarrassing event.
In a way, training pants are like the interim boyfriend. They get you from your breakup with the
diaper to your lifelong relationship with underpants. Like the interim boyfriend, this can either
work splendidly or fail miserably.

When it comes to the training pants, there
are two different kinds: disposable and not. The
popular disposable versions that line your grocery
store aisles have a lot of pluses. They come in dec-
orative colors and styles with your child's favorite
Disney character on the front. They're easy to deal
with, as you just rip them off at the seam and toss
them into the trash. No pulling up and down, and
oh! the mess that comes with that. And finally,
they keep moisture and all that sort of yuckity-
yuck away from Junior's delicate skin, so he can
walk around with a piss-filled diaper for hours
with nary a backwards glance or furrowed brow.

Unfortunately this comfort factor comes with a heavy price tag (not unlike these disposable training pants themselves). For if he's comfortable, he won't have any motivation to use the potty. And after all, you want Junior to want to use the toilet. If he can not only get to wear these cool-looking underpants with a picture of his favorite superhero, and on top of it, is allowed to crap in them and still play in the sandbox for hours on end, he just might want to stay in this blissful state for years to come.

This, along with the expense of disposables, might lead you to the more traditional cotton you're-gonna-have-to-wash-it sort of training pants. These still function as a transition from diaper to underpants, but they aren't so comfortable, and they actually encourage Junior to move through this stage more quickly. Also, they are not the least bit fashion friendly. No space rangers, or cute little bears, or pink mermaids if that's what your little squirt likes. Those fancy "big boy" or "big girls" underpants might seem a little more desirable when your toddler is faced with plain white cotton training pants. More importantly, you might be more motivated to focus on toileting if Junior's training pants weren't so dang convenient.

But I'm still not going to give you my opinion. Rather, I'll give you my pediatrician's: Our beloved Dr. Nancy feels that the disposable training pants, as in "Pull Ups," are a big no-no. Why? Because they aren't really teaching Junior anything. How is he supposed to develop control and good habits if he can unload any time? It goes back to the comfort issue. Standing in a pair of wet cotton briefs is going to send a much stronger message (albeit benign and safe, so you don't need to feel guilty) than standing in a pair of hyperengineered ergonomically designed training pants that are specifically intended to not let your child feel wet. Now of course, Dr. Nancy isn't going to come to your house and wash those nasty-as-nasty-can-be pants. So, in the end, as with most things in life (except for control of the remote during playoff season), the choice is yours.

Other Stuff

As if there weren't enough stuff in your shopping cart already! Along with potty chairs and training pants, you can go on the Internet, or just to your local baby supply or discount store, and spend yourself red on items to potty train your child. Please, try to resist this impulse. People have been doing this for centuries without the use of all the latest gadgets and do-hickies. While you will want to buy stock in Toddler Wipes (which you will be purchasing by the truckload for the rest of your life, as they are the most brilliant invention in the history of mankind), please do not run out and buy buzzers, beepers, alarms, and "pods" (maxi pads for babies) just yet. I'm not saying you can't buy them at all; I'm just giving you advance warning against the panic buy. Chances are, as soon as you spend all that dough on goggles, gloves, and hazardous-waste protective gear, your little one will climb up onto the potty and pee all by himself.

So take a deep breath, do a little research, even try it the old-fashioned way with just a toilet and a smile, and use your money to get yourself a massage. You need it way more than that singing toilet seat (for a list of gadgets and gismos—see the Appendix, page 201).

Potty Mouth

Potty training is an educational experience, and one thing you're going to learn is a whole new language. This language won't impress any high-powered business associates or help you locate your lost luggage at a European airport. Nonetheless, it is quite useful, and you'll find that you'll use it willingly and freely at all places and times, without any regard to how stupid you might sound. This is what we do as desperate parents on a mission to secure continence in our offspring. We speak in the language of the potty.

What's worse, there are a million different dialects of this language, for every family has its own special way of describing body parts and bodily functions. This can make the whole potty-language thing a bit tricky. So bear in mind if you teach Junior to call his penis "Little Peety" because you think it's cute and harmless, just know that he'll be making references to "Little Peety" at preschool, the supermarket, and Grandma's house as well. And while some books (and maybe your pediatrician) will insist you use anatomically correct terminology for your child's intimacies, his preschool teachers and playmates might give him a second look when he announces he needs to "void" or have a "bowel movement."

When teaching your child the language of the potty, keep in mind that he's going to have a difficult enough time just using the potty, let alone pronouncing some of the anatomically correct

> **"** My two-year-old has a doll that she carries with her everywhere and shows off to strangers wherever she goes. All goes fine until they ask what her dolly's name is. You wouldn't believe the expressions when she excitedly tells them that her name is Bagina. **"**
>
> —Alicia

words, like urination and urethra. I don't know of one little girl who doesn't have a "bagina." I mean really, let's just have the "v" legally changed to "b" already, so we're all on the same page for something.

As with many aspects of parenting, there are no hard-and-fast rules governing what words to choose. Over time, your family will develop its own language. It will probably start as something baby-like and evolve into something more mature when the time warrants. Your best bet is to do some listening on the playground. If all of your little tyke's friends have a penis, then penis it is, shocking as that may sound coming out of your baby's adorable little mouth. But chances are that at his age, most of his friends will be sporting a pee-pee, which may sound like a better starting point to you. In the case of potty panic, or complete and total communication breakdown between you and the member of another tribe, use the following translations as a reference.

Excrement-to-English Dictionary

To urinate: void, pee, pee-pee, tinkle, whiz, take a whiz, make sissy, go, go potty, potty, go to the pot, piss, take a piss, take a steaming piss, wee-wee, go wee, go number one, use the can, go to the toilet, make wee-wee

Urine: pee, pee-pee, piss, wee, sissy, number one

To have a bowel movement: defecate, poo, poo-poo, poop, doo, doo-doo, make a doodie, doodle, do a dookie, drop a load, crap, go number two, use the can, do one's business, lay tracks

Stool: a BM, feces, poop, doo-doo, doo, number two, turd, log, Yule log, tootsie roll, piece of crap, big job

To pass gas: break wind, fart, cut the cheese, drive an airbus, let it fly, make an air biscuit

Vagina: bagina, coochie, privates, woo-woo

Penis: pecker, pee-pee, wiener, weenie, weenus, Johnson, little [fill in boy's name], wanger, thing, thingy, it, ding-dong, peter

Going without underwear: freestyle, free and easy, commando style

Gluteus maximus: bottom, butt, derriere, tush, tushie, heinie, tuckus

Chapter 2

let's get this potty started!

Before we officially begin teaching your kid how to use the potty, we have to be in sync about what to actually call this process. You'll notice that some books refer to it as "toilet learning" while others simply call it "toilet training." In my opinion, no matter what you call it, it's all a lot of hard work, and you have enough to deal with without needing to be politically correct. "Potty learning" may sound more soft and cuddly, but I'm going to stick with the traditional "potty training" because . . . well . . . because it's my book, and I can call it whatever I want. So let's move on.

Let's assume that right now you're at Point A. Your child is showing significant signs of potty-training readiness, and you've added a wing to your home to store the necessary potty-training accessories. The question now remains, how do you get your child from Point A to Point B? Or better yet, what exactly is Point B? In an attempt to avoid confusion, let me spell it out for you:

Point B (a.k.a. Your New Goal in Life)

- Your child tells you she has to go.
- She walks, crawls, or Broadway shuffles into the bathroom.
- She pulls down her pants.
- She goes inside the potty.
- She wipes the affected area.
- She pulls her pants back up.
- She flushes.
- She washes and dries her hands.
- You buy yourself a lobster dinner.

I know that right now this scenario seems as far away as people forgetting about Tom Cruise's incident of jumping on Oprah's couch, but trust me when I say that there are dozens of ways to get to that lobster dinner. You just need to decide which route is the best one for you and your family.

Regardless of the method you do decide to use, don't tell anyone your plan. Remember the lesson you learned after you and your spouse spent months agonizing over a name for you child? Then you made the terrible mistake of actually telling people what the name was? Those well-wishers had no problem telling you exactly how wrong you were in your decision. And they'll have no problem telling you exactly how wrong you are now. It's just the way people operate. We're a culture of know-it-alls and boundary crossers. The more private the matter, the more heated the debate. And there's nothing more controversial in life than parenting, and nothing more private than the potty.

Most importantly, stay away from your mother-in-law until this entire process is complete (or maybe until your kid gets his own apartment). For no matter what you do, she'll be shocked at how you're doing it and disappointed in your son for marrying you in the first place. She'll click her tongue in disgust and shake her head in indignant disapproval. And you'll most certainly end up in your local penitentiary with a murder rap on your head. Then again, that would get you out of having to potty train. Hmmmm. Something to consider.

You just need to know going in that whatever method of potty training you decide to employ, there will be setbacks, accidents, successes and failures, laughter and tears and all that good stuff in between that goes along with raising an actual human being. It's also important to know that it's always okay to change your game plan in "mid-stream." Just like on the LA freeway, there are many ways to get from Point A to Point B. Some of the most popular potty-training methods are listed below to help you ease on down the road. So read on, compatriot. You can do this! Just follow the yellow brick road to a toilet-trained toddler. And just hope that the bricks are yellow because someone actually painted them that way.

Potty Training in the Fantasy World

By now, you've probably read a few books on babies and parenting. (If you're a new mom, chances are you've read the entire section at your local bookstore.) And if you're reading this book, most likely you're desperate (and definitely very, very smart). But if you're anything like me, you've discovered that the babies described in these parenting books do not exist. Nothing is ever as easy in life as it is in print. And your baby rarely does what the book says she should. Babies rarely give up their blankies if you offer them a sticker. They rarely eat what you put in front of them, even if you give it a funny name. And they'll rarely use the potty, no matter how fun you try to make it out to be.

I have a theory that the people who write these books make it look easy on purpose. They are in fact creating a fictional world in order to instill confidence in new parents so that they'll believe that they can actually pull off this whole child-rearing business. It's a parenting bait-and-switch con game, if you will. If they didn't do this, if they told you what it was really like to raise a baby, most people would load up on birth control and stop having babies altogether. And since pediatricians write the majority of these books, they know that they'd soon be out of business.

Having said that, I can firmly attest that parenting is doable—just maybe not in the free-and-easy way described in a lot of books lining your library shelves. This is especially true when it comes to potty training. Nevertheless, in the spirit of optimism, and hell, an all-out belief in miracles, I'll go ahead and outline this fantasy method of potty training as it appears in books:

- You supply your child with an adequate potty chair or potty seat.
- Your child becomes interested in the potty and wants to sit on it.
- You put your child on the potty chair at the same time every day so sitting on it becomes part of a routine.
- Throughout the day, you ask your child to try to use the potty and remind her to tell you if she needs to go.
- When your child successfully uses the potty, you reward her with praise. If your child does not succeed, you do not reprimand or punish.
- When your child has successfully used the potty several times, switch to cotton underwear.
- Keep up your potty training even when you are away from home.
- When your child is consistently using the potty during the day, and the night diaper is often dry in the mornings, it's time to take off the diapers at night.

For those of you who have already begun potty training, I'll give you a minute to laugh this off. I know. It's a good one. For those of you who haven't begun potty training, I'll give you a moment to savor the fantasy. And while you're at it, you might as well imagine that Brad Pitt is your husband and you can still fit into your size six jeans.

Okay, time's up! Now I'll tell you how it really happens:

- You buy your kid a potty chair and place it optimistically in your bathroom.
- Your child becomes interested in the potty and wants to use it as a container for her Lego's.
- You search the house at the same time every day for the missing potty chair, while your kid pees all over herself. As a matter of routine, you find the potty chair in front of the kitchen cupboard where you keep the cookies.
- Throughout the day, you beg your child to use the potty, offering her candy and cartoons in hopes that she'll tell you when she needs to go. You place the potty chair in front of the TV.

- When your child successfully uses the potty, you call all the people in your phone book and tell them that your child is potty trained.
- You fold and refold the cotton underwear that lies untouched in your child's dresser drawer.
- You use the excuse of being away from home to not potty train—after all, those public restrooms are filthy.
- When you see that your child is consistently not using the potty during the day, you don't even consider night training. Give the entire venture up for a couple of months. Make yourself a consolation pitcher of vodka gimlets. And use the freaking potty-chair as a planter in the back yard.

Incentives, Bribes, and the Dreaded C-Word

Time to get down to brass diaper pins. If you're the proud owner of a toddler, chances are you've come to appreciate the power of incentives in making your home run smoothly. An incentive is the reward you give your child upon completion of said goal. "If you eat all your dinner, then you can have a popsicle." "If you put your toys away, then you can watch Barney." Better yet, "If you let Mommy have ten uninterrupted minutes all to herself without any whining, demands, or tantrums, then you can spend all day at the arcade." Whoops! Okay, so maybe I pushed it a bit, but you get my drift. The idea is to motivate your child in a healthy manner to achieve a desired, reasonable result.

Incentives are not the same as bribes, which should be avoided at all costs. A bribe is an incentive in response to the word "No." For example: "Please drink your milk." "No!" "If you drink your milk, then I'll give you candy." If this sounds familiar, then you are in deep doo-doo, for this is a very bad habit. If fact, you're setting yourself up for a long life with a spoiled slacker. Toddlers who are raised on bribes often turn into children who can get by with the bare minimum amount of effort. Who can blame them? They've been taught that "No" will get them a prize. Nothing is expected of them. These children inevitably grown into adults who spend all day at the arcade, have a hard time holding jobs, never have meaningful relationships, and live with their mommies until they're old enough to cash their

Social Security checks. For the love of Sponge-Bob, if you ever want grandchildren, don't bribe your kid.

Of course, what motivates your child to use the potty correctly is entirely up to your child. There is no set formula for children, as they are all as different and individual as soap bubbles. Some children are driven solely by the admiration and approval of their parents. A few words of praise are the only incentive that they need. If these are your children, bravo. Give them a pat on the back for me, and say hello to your pet unicorn while you're at it.

Other children require something a bit more concrete than just a hug and a kiss. This is where the old sticker chart may come in handy. Every tinkle on the toilet gets them a star. A certain number of stars gets them a prize—like a crazy straw for them and mani-pedi for mommy. This method might look good on paper, literally, but there's a problem. Most kids (I'm not saying all, and I'm certainly not saying yours) who are of potty-training age do not have the ability to grasp this concept. They don't understand counting or waiting, and they certainly aren't the bastions of good sportsmanship. So rather than "I need to use the potty, dear Mother," you'll more likely get, "I want my prize *now*! Waaaaaaaaah!" And if you're like me, you'll end up with stars stuck all over your bathroom walls and a puddle of pee in the corner.

By far, the most desperate "incentive" of all—and I hesitate to even use the term "incentive" here—is the dreaded C-word: candy. Bluntly stated, you give your kid a sugary treat if she uses the potty. Sounds horrible. Is horrible. Happens all the time. That's because it can work. But for the sake of your future, and your child's future teeth, can we please do everything possible to stay away from this incentive. Not only is it bad for your child's physical health, it's gotta be bad for her mental health as well. There's just something fundamentally wrong with putting a fattening morsel in a kid's mouth when she excretes something out of her bottom. If you need a stronger

> **"** Before I started potty training, I swore I'd never be like those mothers who gave their kids M&M's whenever they used the potty. But by the end, I was so desperate, I had moved past the M&M's and was up to the $7 white-chocolate Easter chicks from Williams Sonoma. **"**
>
> —Sue

incentive than a sticker, how about a shiny new crystal, a coloring book, a model car, or a good old-fashioned hug?

Better yet, how about forgoing incentives altogether? Some might argue that incentives are just setting your kid up for failure. If she is unable or not ready to use the potty, she's not going to get the coveted prize. Then all you'll have is a tiny tot with a wet diaper, a broken heart, and a countdown to a tantrum so bad that you'll want to reverse time and claim a headache on the night you conceived. By using incentives, you're in essence rewarding your child for having a bodily function. And where does it end? "Here sweetie, a diamond tennis bracelet for passing gas." Remember, you could be at this for a long time. You must ask yourself going in whether this is a precedent you want to set. Aren't you tired enough as it is without having to take on the new title of Potty Prize Patrol?

Keep in mind that your child will be potty trained with or without incentives. Consider that the best course of action might be to let nature take its course, without all the bells and whistles and chocolate-coated treats. And in the end, and I mean the very end, when the work is done and the sun is setting on the horizon, then you and

Junior can both sit back and enjoy that celebratory hot-fudge sundae.

New Age Craze-Y

Before we sample the array from the smorgasbord of potty-training techniques, I want to take a minute to discuss the new trend in training. It goes by a couple of names: "infant potty training" (or IPT) and "elimination communication" (or EC). Chances are you've seen or heard about this method somewhere. After all, the folks who brought us this New Age belief have probably dropped a sweet load on publicity and promotion, and therefore, it's in the news. I myself saw a segment on it on the *Today* show back in October of 2005, and Matt Lauer had to do his all-around best to keep from cracking up.

It should come as no surprise that not all societies embrace our Western methods of getting our kids to use the can. This new movement in "movements" is based on the belief system of other cultures like Asia, Africa, and South America. Believe it or not, this method of potty training teaches babies to start using the potty from infancy! Yes, you heard me right. Infancy! Due to cultural ideas, environmental concerns, or just a plain lack of local 7-11's for those 3 A.M. diaper runs, these cultures devised another technique that seems to work quite well for them. But now those beliefs have been imported, and New Age mommies want their babies to use the potty on cue from the get go as well. Never mind that these little blobs of flesh can't even manage to fall asleep by themselves, or burp without vomiting.

If you want to partake in this trend, you should plan on potty training your child somewhere from birth to around five months. You should forgo diapers, throw away your diaper pail, and go straight to the potty. And hey, while you're at it, why don't you start prepping your infant for his SATs!

Just for kicks, let me tell you a little bit about how this method works. You, the mommy, wait for a signal from your little blob that he has to do his business. Then you race like a hyper cartoon character to put his tiny tushie on a teeny weenie bowl and give him an audible cue, like "Sssss." But the question remains, what is the sign that you should be looking for? One if by land, two if by pee? Sure, a baby may grimace and grunt before he drops a load, but I've never seen any warning signs for a tinkle. And the rare smile of relief after the event ain't gonna do you one lick of good.

Even if your gifted child does display some sort of heads-up warning sign, you'd have to stare at your kid all day while waiting for it to make an appearance. And frankly, what new parent has the time to sit around all day watching the baby like she was a bomb waiting to go off? We barely have time to inhale. For heaven's sake, put a diaper on the kid, put her in her vibrating chair, and go take your weekly shower.

Even with all of these hindrances, a small section of our society has actually embraced this method of potty training. These mommies feel that training a child this way is kinder and less traumatic, and that it creates a strong bond of trust between parent and child. Me? I think all it does is create a lot of laundry. The reasoning here, in my opinion, is just plain silly. Honestly, what's so traumatic about potty training for a kid in the first place? There are so many other legitimately upsetting things for a little one to stress over, like itchy tags, putting away toys, and having to give up their binkies. In fact, potty training is no doubt the best time a toddler can have. He gets Mommy's undivided attention while being read book upon book while sitting comfortably on a shiny new chair. Trauma? What trauma? Potty training is the next best thing to a Disney cruise.

Still, if you insist on giving it a try, if you worry that otherwise you'll be missing out on some transcendent parenting experience, then by all means, go for it! Just remember to take up your rugs, reseal your floors, encase your furniture in plastic, and Scotch Guard all of your clothing. Don't forget to keep an extra bowl in your purse for those trips to the bank or the market. And while you're at it, you better go out and get yourself a whole new circle of friends because everyone you know in life thus far is going to think you're a total freak. And who can blame them? After all, you'll be following your kid around with a bowl under her butt like she's a cigarette with an ash about to fall.

Who knows? After months of effort, you might be rewarded with a little turd in your cup. You may develop a bond with your child that will last a lifetime. You may foster a healthy body image and engender communication skills far beyond your child's young years. Yes, you may even be rewarded with a child who is fully potty trained by the time she learns to find her thumb. But chances are better that after all your effort, the only thing that you'll be rewarded with is a kid who's covered in crap, a house that smells like a litter box, and not one clean bowl left for your cereal in the morning.

What Your Mother-in-Law Doesn't Know

I'm lucky. My mother-in-law had eleven grand-kids by the time my daughter was born. By then, she was so busy babysitting and making cookies that she had neither the time nor the energy to give me unwanted advice about how to raise my kid. But I know most of you aren't as fortunate as to have married into a family the size of Scranton. Because of this, you're bombarded by "advice" everyday. And potty training is the Super Bowl of mother-in-law wisdom.

The reason that your mother-in-law feels so entitled to nag is that she claims that she got her kids out of diapers by the time they were two years old. So when she sees her four-year-old grandson wearing Pull-Ups underneath the cute sailor suit she gave him, the floodgate of mother-in-law advice is opened. Deep down, you don't believe that she's such a gifted potty trainer. You're convinced that her kids were cutting wisdom teeth when they finished training and she just forgot, like how she "forgets" your birthday and "forgets" to mention you in her yearly Christmas letter. I'm sorry to tell you this, but she's right. Chances are that she's telling you the truth.

Before the 1960s, it was unusual for a three-year-old to still be in diapers. If this did happen, this kid's mom was talked about more than the new pornographic invention called a bikini. What your mother-in-law doesn't take into account is one enormous "benefit" she had in her favor: She potty trained before the advent of disposable diapers.

Disposable diapers were invented in 1949 by a woman named Marion Donovan. Marion experimented by wrapping cloth diapers in cut-up shower curtains. She packaged her idea under the name of "Boater," and they became a hit at Saks Fifth Avenue. Later, she sold her patent for a million dollars. Holy crap!

By the 1960s, Procter and Gamble was hawking disposable diapers on commercials featuring the respected pediatrician T. Berry Brazelton. The ingenious marketing plan was to push the idea of "hands-off potty training," thereby keeping toddlers in diapers years longer and selling more diapers. As anyone who's ever bought breast enhancer cream knows, people believe what they hear, and now, years later, it's rare to find a two-year-old who's potty trained.

It's no big surprise that disposable diapers create an enormous delay in potty training. They're much more comfortable to wear. They're so absorbent that the child can pee on herself all day and be none the wiser. Take that same kid, put her in a cloth diaper, and she'll be wet and miserable. If you've ever peed in your cotton underwear when you coughed (and who amongst us has not?), you know just what I'm talking about.

So even though you resent your mother-in-law for her unannounced visits and for turning your husband into a spineless wimp whenever she's around, she is right about getting her kid to train earlier than yours. But don't worry. Even though she got her kids out of diapers before you, she'll be in them before you as well, and that may bring you a wee bit of comfort.

The Dr. Phil Method

Unless you've been living in a cave high up in the mountains of the West Indies, you've heard of the omnipresent Dr. Phil. We all know him. Some of us love him. And some of us think he's a space monkey sent down to Earth from the mother ship Oprah to bend the minds of our human race using subliminal messages hidden in million-dollar catch phrases like "How's that workin' for ya?" and "You have to name it to claim it."

I mean really, have you seen this guy in action? There's something about him that doesn't make sense. How does any doctor who uses his first name for a last name get to be so rich and so famous so quickly? How can he solve every problem from incest to infidelity in between commercial breaks? Everyone just blindly follows his proclamations and commands, like horror-film housewives wandering zombie-like through life. And why, I ask, do women fall under his magic charm? It's not like he's George Clooney or Mathew Broderick (my personal favorite). For goodness sake, if you're going to worship someone, at least let him be a hottie.

To top it off, along with his methods for life, love, marriage, divorce, child rearing, weight loss, and Neilson ratings, this gabfest guru also has his own sure-fire method for potty training. It's based on the philosophy that, against all instinctual tendencies on your part, potty training needs to be a positive experience. (Perhaps this is how it works on Planet Oprah.) Here it is in a nutshell:

1. Buy an anatomically correct "drink and wet" doll. On Earth, this is a doll with an opening in both its pie hole and pee hole.

2. Dress your dolly in "big kid" underwear. On Earth, these are white cotton briefs or panties that you purchase by the boatload at Target, or for a fortune at baby specialty stores.

3. Have your child teach Dolly how to use the potty. On Earth, we call this "role playing." We also do this when practicing for a job interview, accepting our Oscar in front of the medicine cabinet mirror, or preparing to tell our spouse that we put a dent in the car. Give Dolly a name, give her a drink, and watch her pee into the potty.

4. Now that Dolly is potty trained, Dolly gets a party! On Earth, we really like to go for it in the party department: hats, horns, decorations, music, maybe even a cookie or a margarita for mommy. Lavish that doll with attention so that your child knows that making in the potty is "a good thing" (oh wait, wrong space monkey). Make sure

your child knows that when she is potty trained, she too will get a party, and can call her favorite superhero. In the meantime, you get to play party time with your little one, which is quite enchanting.

NOTE: Do not make the mistake of throwing a party each and every time Dolly uses the potty or you'll end up broke, exhausted, ass-drunk from margaritas, and with a child on the fast track to a lifestyle like Lindsay Lohan's.

5. Now it's your child's turn. Ceremoniously put away the diapers and put "big kid" underwear on your little one.

6. Ply your child with liquids and take her to the bathroom ten times in a row: On Planet Oprah, "ten" is a significant number infused with power and deep meaning. Here, it's just an old, if not charming little movie starring Dudley Moore—but out of respect, we'll stick with it. Ask your child if she needs to go to the potty. If you get a "No," don't worry. Your child is full of fluids and will have to go soon enough.

7. If your little one has an accident, don't scold or punish. This is true for any planet. Just walk her to the potty, take off the wet underpants, and place her on the pot. Do it

ten times. This supposedly builds up muscle memory. I actually just think it builds up tantrums.

8. Once your child makes tinkle in the potty, it's party time! Not only is there a party, but your child can call his favorite superhero. On Dr. Phil's home planet, I imagine this would be Oprah herself. On Earth, any superhero will do: Spiderman, Batman, Sponge Bob, Barbie, you get the picture. (You'll need to enlist the help of friend to play the hero unless you have really good connections.)

Note that if you happen to have a strong-willed child who doesn't want anyone telling her what to do (in other words, a three-year-old), this approach might not be the best one for you. But if you put your love and trust in Dr. Phil, then go ahead and give it a go. According to the great Dr. Phil himself, if you follow these instructions, you can have your child potty trained *in one day*. That's a mighty big promise, sir. But then again, Dr. Phil is a mighty big guy. And personally, I don't want to mess with that.

The "Make Someone Else Do It" Method

This method is by far my favorite method of potty training. As the name suggests, this method involves getting anyone but you to potty train your child. And while you may think I'm tugging your chain, I'm not, because in a weird way it makes sense. Your life is fraught with struggles between you and your child—from bedtime to bath time to dinner time, it's all hard time. And trust me when I tell you that potty training can be the worst time of all. The last thing you need is to add these kinds of severe battle scars to your life.

You and your child are so intimately and emotionally linked that an issue as personal and sensitive as potty training can threaten to detonate your relationship, like a volcano waiting to erupt. Stepping out of the picture, and letting someone else step into your place, could be just the ticket for both you and your kid. Your child will probably not be able to manipulate someone else the way she manipulates you. We see this every day in schools, day cares, and Gymborees across the country. Your child will perform and act in ways that you never knew she could, as long as she has a nonpartisan audience. And, sorry to say, another voice might carry more weight than your own. It's just a fact of life: From infancy on, kids zone out their parents. Get over it—this isn't about ego. It's about poop. And you want to do whatever you can to get it into the potty.

Conversely, for the love of Barney, don't feel guilty about not being the almighty one to potty train your child. You carried that little dickens in your belly for nine long months, then pushed it out a hole that's the size of a shiny new quarter. You've given up your sleep, your sex drive, your figure, your freedom, and your life for that tyke, and if you don't feel like climbing this mountain, nobody will blame you. And if they do, then don't invite them to your Christmas party next year. End of story.

So if the idea of this technique sounds appealing, you have essentially four avenues to take. Pick one.

Avenue A: Your Husband

We probably all have one or two friends whose husbands completely co-parent their children. They are true partners in the endeavor of child rearing. These men actually go to the market, change diapers, take the kid to the pediatrician, and even cook a meal from time to time. It is these men who would be good candidates to take over the potty-training process. They have the patience, love, time, and the right balance of female hormones in their system to make this a feasible option. These sensitive dudes would most likely be happy to assume the responsibility for training their offspring out of appreciation for their wives, for all their hard work and sacrifice, and for the pure joy of participating in yet another milestone in their child's life (cue sappy Celine Dion love song).

Personally, I've seen many men who believe co-parenting is for sissies. Diapers are not to be touched, a market is a place to trade stocks, and dinner should be on the table at six. And while I was able to drag my husband to our baby's early doctor's appointments, her first shot sent him running out the front door, never to be seen in that neighborhood again. Some part of me feels that on some level, I chose a man just like my father, who didn't help out much in the baby department. But the main part of me thinks that this is how most men are. It's easy and convenient for them to relegate the screaming, messy, and downright ugly parts of parenting to the womenfolk. Society has been doing it this way for centuries, and if it means they don't have to deal with a poopie bottom, then all the better for them.

If this sounds the least bit familiar, then forget about having your husband potty train your child. It will lead only to frustration for both daddy and baby and, in turn, more frustration for you. But if you have one of those incredible men who clears the table and knows how to get rid of bathroom scum, then count your lucky stars and give me one of his cheek cells so that I can get him cloned!

Avenue B: A Grandmother

One day, I overheard an old German woman speaking of her younger days in the land of Oom Pah Pah. She said that in Europe, when it was time to potty train the young ones, "Grandma vould vatch for zee scrunchy face, zen put zee little vun on zee pot." Translation: The grandma was in charge of the potty-training department.

The main problem with this technique is that it requires an actual grandmother. And not just any grandmother will do. You'll need a grandmother who has the time to sit around all day staring at your child. This means a grandmother who does not have a job, friends, or a life of her own. And in the United States, good, bad, or indifferent, a lot of grandmothers work, are married, and live very full, active, and independent lives—those selfish biddies! I say it's time that all we new moms move to Europe, where the grandmothers live to serve us, and better yet, serve our children. Where, at the end of the day, our house is clean, the family meal is prepared, and our baby is completely potty trained. This is where a good grandmother knows her place in the world!

Even if you did happen to find an unemployed, single grandmother who was willing to take over this dirty task, the chances are high that she would have her own opinions as to how potty training should be conducted. She may believe in scolding or humiliation. Even worse, she could be your husband's mother, and that scenario is already fraught with plenty of complications, drama, and prospective violence. What are the odds that your mother or mother-in-law shares your own vision as to how your child should be raised? Just think back on their views on discipline, thumb sucking, and premarital sex, and you'll have your answer.

But if you find that someone you know meets the requisite requirements for this method, consider yourself to be the luckiest mom alive. Throw some bratwurst on the barbi, put away your lederhosen (unless you and your hubby are into that sort of thing) and celebrate! Oh, and I wouldn't mind one of her cheek cells as well. What? A girl can never have too much help in the potty-training department!

Avenue C: Your Nanny or Babysitter

I know this may sound strange at first, but the concept is not much different than those dog trainers who will take your brand-new puppy for a few days and bring him back fully housebroken. This method is especially well suited for the working mom who isn't home to do the dirty deed. While most day-care centers will take babies in diapers, most preschools will not, which means that your nanny or baby-sitter will have to do it before preschool begins.

As long as you deal with the morale issue and the guilt of being a lousy mommy, this situation can work quite well. If your nanny or sitter's only responsibility is your child, she should have the time and attention span to "watch for the scrunchy face." Bear in mind that you'll have to talk about how you'd like her to handle potty training, as she may have her own way of doing things. Since you won't be there to micro manage, you need to feel confident that she knows exactly what you want her to do. Once you begin this messy chapter in your child's life, you'll want to make sure that your entire household is on the same page. It will only serve to confuse Junior if nanny/sitter potty trains one way during the day, Mommy does it differently at night, and Daddy doesn't do it at all.

Keep in mind that most nannies and babysitters may not want to take on this responsibility. They feel like they're already doing a lot just caring for your child and often cleaning your house to boot. So if you're preparing to delve into the potty-training world and are asking for their help, it might be a good time to give old Helga, or cute little Caitlin, a nice bonus that's worthy compensation for the task you're asking them to do . . . like a brand-new car!

Avenue D: Your Six-Year-Old

Believe it or not, this is probably the most promising of all your options. If Little Petunia happens to have an older sibling, chances are high that Little Petunia reveres said older sibling (in spite of how the older sibling feels about the younger one). This being the case, Little Petunia will want to copy everything that her older sibling does—from throwing temper tantrums to saying bad words to using the potty.

If your first child adores your second child, recruiting your eldest for the task of potty training should be a cakewalk. But if you're like most of us, and your first child wants to flush your second child down the toilet, special tactics might be in order. Offer your older child a special treat for taking Little "P" to the toilet over and over again. Don't expect your eldest to do the actual dirty work of cleaning up or wiping dirty parts (sorry, child labor went out ages ago). Still, if your elder child "counsels" the younger sibling, helps her onto the potty, and sits with her, a normally highly charged situation can change into something that's fun and fruitful.

Take advantage of this peer pressure now and enjoy it while you can. At this tender young age, it comes in quite handy, not only for toilet training but for getting your younger child to eat her veggies and get dressed all by herself. As your kids age, this peer pressure will be used for evil instead of good. It will be the reason your youngest is watching R-rated movies, visiting online chat rooms, and getting a tattoo of her biker boyfriend on her heinie.

“ I'll never forget when my four-year-old son took my two-year-old daughter into the bathroom, set up her potty chair, sat her down, then climbed onto the toilet himself. He closed the door and told me, "We don't need you." As I was getting over my heartbreak, my kids emerged from the bathroom with two happy faces, two clean behinds, and two little presents in two different bowls. ”

—Margaret

The "Do Nothing" Method

Now that I've told you about every method under the sun for potty training your child, I'll tell you what finally worked for me: absolutely nothing. That's right. Zero, zip, nada, zilch.

With my daughter, I fell for the social, familial, and Martha Stewart pressures of having to do everything perfectly in the parenting department; from needing her to look fabulous at all times, to using utensils, and to be potty trained by two and a half—at the latest. I tried everything to get her potty trained: positive reinforcement, stickers, colorful potty seats, musical potty seats, nudity, role-playing, bribes, and finally, all-out screaming. Then, when she was three and a half, and in spite of my best efforts, she hoisted her pink princess-clad tushie onto the potty and peed all by herself.

Some research shows that no matter when you start potty training, toddlers tend to decide they want to control their bladders and bowels all by themselves by around three and a half. This is when they generally develop a desire to be clean and to want to grow up and "fit in." Your child will start to notice the white cotton cartoon character underpants in her drawer, and she'll tire of her bulky wet diapers. Preschool also gives an assist in the potty-training arena because she'll start to notice her older friends using the toilets after snack time and want to fit in with the crowd.

You can begin potty training whenever you choose, but chances are that no matter when you start, your child will be fully potty trained about this age. Remember, a toddler's success at potty training will be because of your toddler's efforts—not yours. So unless you enjoy the bazillion trips to the bathroom a day, the stinky potty chairs, the tears, the frustrations, the accidents and the aggravation, why kill yourself? Leave the diapers on, take the pressure off, and let nature take its course.

The point is, when it comes to a battle of wills, the toddler is going to win. You cannot force your child to use the toilet before she is physically able, and trying to do so is inviting defiance. In fact, the power struggle you create with this issue could quite possible delay potty training. You'll no doubt realize how effective this method is by the time your second baby rolls around. By then, you'll be so busy with the endless chores and so exhausted from the midnight feedings that you'll barely even remember to feed your firstborn, let alone worry about trivial things like potty training. Somewhere around your kid's second birthday, you'll throw a dusty old potty chair on the bathroom floor, give her a few pointers, and call it a day. Whenever it's convenient, you'll let her watch you go potty, or, if you have a boy, his dad will show him the standing-up trick. Yes, by the time the next child comes around, the one who will teach him to use the potty will be good ol' Mother Nature. Heck, she's done a fine job with things like the waterfalls and sunsets, so she's certainly qualified to do it.

Chapter 3

urine for some fun now!

Statistics show that about half of all marriages fail, that four out of five dentists prefer sugarless gum, and that most toddlers conquer going number one before moving on to the more difficult psychological battle of going number two. That's why our first bodily function to focus on is urination and the problems that you may face when you try to get your kid to go wee-wee without a diaper.

To the naïve, this task may appear to be quite simple. Just sit your kid down on the potty chair whenever the urge hits him, and he will go pee. To paraphrase an old Kevin Costner baseball movie, "Buy it and he will pee."

But to the educated parent, or anyone who's ever gone through a home remodel, things are never as easy as they seem. In reality, keeping a child dry is as complex and multifaceted a problem as today's ever-changing tax codes, consisting of issues like the challenges of boy training versus girl training, pants on pants off, sitting versus standing, and a whole slough of other new and exciting child-rearing issues—all for the sake of getting a little tinkle from your little tyke. Where to begin, you might ask? Why, at the beginning, of course.

Connecting the Urge with the Purge

Potty training is all about mastering new skills and facing new challenges. The first and biggest of these has got to be getting a young pisser to connect the actual sensation of having to pee with the act of peeing itself. In the past, there was never a need for your child to identify the urge to pee. Peeing was like any other naturally occurring toddler function, like breathing or projectile vomiting. It just happened when it happened, and Mommy took care of the rest. But now that your child is ready to climb aboard the Potty Train, urge and urination need to be addressed as two very distinct and separate steps. For the train won't make it out of the station unless your child can recognize the feeling of a full bladder. Here are a few ways to assist your child in knowing if he has to go:

- Timing is everything. Keep an eye on your child's natural potty rhythms. If your child pees like clockwork every day right after Zoboomafu, then intercept it. Put him on the potty during the end credits and try to catch the pee before the stream begins.
- If Junior wakes up dry from a nap, put him on the pot the moment he opens his eyelids. There's a good chance that his tank is full and he's moments away from bursting.
- If you put him on the pot and nothing happens, turn on the faucet and let it flow like a pee-like stream. Running the tap is an old trick, but it works. (Trust me, you'll be pushing Junior off the seat so you can get on). If still nothing happens, then abandon the attempt. Repeat, abandon attempt. You don't want to start a power struggle. Remember, we're only tying to get Junior to connect the sensation with the action.

NOTE: I know that some of you like to turn on the faucet full blast, but potty training shouldn't be hard on the environment. We've already filled up enough landfills with disposable diapers.

- Be grateful to your child for reporting an accident. Take it as progress. Better yet, if your child has an accident on the way to the potty, praise him and consider it a big success that he knew that he had to go in the first place.
- Finally, resist the temptation to ask him a hundred million times a day, "Do you have to go to the bathroom?" You're trying to teach your child to recognize his own urge, and unless you want to be the wacky mom following her sixteen-year-old son around at football games asking if he has to make tinkle-tink, you need to give your kid some space.

Once a toddler is able to identify the sensation of having to pee, then you're good to go. Just remember the following:

- It's easier to have a pee accident than a poo accident as pee is aerodynamically designed to move faster than poo. Ergo, make sure a potty is handy at all times. If you have a large or two-story house, you may need to buy potties in bulk and place them strategically around the house.

- Keep Junior bare bottomed as much as possible, and be on puddle patrol. There's nothing worse than walking barefoot through a puddle of pee, except perhaps walking barefoot on a snail. I did that once, and the crunch and slimy sensation has stayed with me for a lifetime. I know you may be tempted to spread newspaper on the floor, but that might invite participation from Fido and you already have enough to deal with.

- Try not to take diapers away altogether too soon. If it turns out that your kid isn't ready to potty train yet, it could sap his self-esteem to be put back in diapers after he thought they were gone for good.

- At the same time, be careful not to let your kid's potty chair become his new security object or it will make traveling quite difficult (and visits to Grandma quite heated).

- Finally, toddlers pee all day long, so expect successes and failures. Eventually the successes will overtake the failures.

The Trouble with Boys

Boys may have an easier time than girls with things like upper body strength and growing facial hair, but when it comes to peeing, we have them sitting down. In the scheme of things, girls get off pretty easy in the bathroom department. With us, it's no muss, no fuss. Sure, we have lots of nooks and crannies to clean, which makes each poopie diaper change as difficult as detailing your car, but at least potty training can be much easier to master. That's because boys have some unique problems to deal with.

The first problem is the whole physiological issue that boys have, which can cause them to train much later than girls. Also, sometimes their little bladders mature a bit more slowly than their female counterparts. (I could make a joke here about the aptitude of the male species as a whole, but that's a matter for another book.) Boys may also have equipment issues to deal with that may cause their urine stream to spray or go off in a different direction from where they aim. This of course would warrant a trip to the doctor's office, but not before you make a video of your son trying to pee in the potty and hitting the nearby family collie instead. If you're lucky, this could warrant an easy $10,000 on *America's Funniest Home Videos.*

Boys also have more fun peeing than girls do, which may make concentrating far more difficult. This fun is due to a boy's unique ability to make a pee fountain. When a boy first realizes that he has such a gift, he'll want to do it all the time, just like Tabitha when she first realized she had her mom Samantha's witch-like abilities. But instead of wiggling his nose and making toys float around a room, a boy will whip out his ding-dong and make a glorious shimmering stream. Whether it be at parties, in parks, or in front of the mailman, your little pumpkin is never far from taking an al fresco whiz and showing off this magical gift. Dealing with this fascination is a tough call. Sure, you want to encourage his potty independence, but it can become quite embarrassing when he waters the nearby bougainvillea at your Mother's Day brunch.

Another challenge when training a little boy is that you're immediately faced with the issue of sitting versus standing. Talk to your husband about this dilemma right off the bat, as he will most likely have an opinion. Generally, monkey see monkey do, and if Daddy-monkey sits, Baby-monkey will want to sit right along beside him.

Personally, I'd avoid the whole sitting scenario if at all possible (that is, unless it's accompanied by a poop). First of all, if your son sits, you have to deal with the "loose cannon" (so to speak). Unless he points his cannon down, it can shoot anywhere, and most frequently does. More importantly, if he stands when he goes wee-wee, that's one less worry for his precious little tush when using a public restroom. And mammas, you know just what I'm talking about.

If you do decide to go with the standing position, it might be easier to start with the potty chair and graduate to the big boy toilet when his legs are a little bit longer. If you go directly to the big time, just make sure you have a sturdy step stool so the little guy can reach the bowl.

A good trick of the tinkle trade is to make the standing position into a game. Toss a few Cheerios into the bowl and have your little Billy the Kid aim and shoot for the floating bull's eyes. It's lots of fun, and better yet, he'll beg you to use the potty again and again and again. In fact, the makers of Cheerios should realize that a huge percentage of their sales is due to this technique and use it as part of their advertising strategy. "Cheerios—a healthy cereal and an excellent target for tinkle!" This "aim and shoot" game also helps the wee-wee from missing the toilet rim, the floor, and most importantly, your new Italian leather boots. Tell your son to watch his aim and focus, focus, focus. Now I know little boys have the attention spans of gnats, but he must pay attention to his flowing pee or you're sure to end up with a fine mess. If he's midstream and suddenly turns around to look at something far more interesting, it's all over . . . everything!

Next, Obi Wan, along with standing and peeing comes another great lesson you must pass on to your young Skywalker. You must teach him how to deal with the jiggle drops. These drops of pee are part and parcel of the male urinary experience. The bottom line is that boys don't wipe.

❝ I was at McDonald's with my son, Justin, and we were about to sit down at a table. As I was taking him out of his stroller, I noticed that he had his penis out of his pants. Before I could stick it back in, he made a pee fountain and peed all over himself—and me! Mortified, I called my husband in tears. But instead of trying to make me feel better, all he did was laugh and say it was the funniest thing he's ever heard. Men! **❞**

—Elisabeth

They jiggle off the excess. And you want these drops to land inside the potty. If they happen to miss and land—God forbid—on the toilet seat, what do you do, girls? That's right. You teach him how to wipe them off and save their future wives from having to do this humiliating task day after day, week after week, as long as they both shall live.

Which brings me to the most important aspect of pee training a boy: etiquette. All right moms, here's your chance. You're growing a man here, so let's take this opportunity to do it right. Your future daughter-in-law will thank you. Right from the get go, you want to teach your boy the following potty manners:

Five Steps to Perfect Potty Propriety

1. Lift the lid and the seat before peeing (and make sure they stay up to prevent that loud and potentially painful slam).
2. Keep the pee inside the potty.
3. Wipe off any stray jiggle drops that land on the rim or elsewhere.
4. Put the seat back down.
5. Flush!

Also, when dealing with poop, it's also important to teach your son to wipe effectively so as to save their future daughter-in-law the most unpleasant chore of pretreating skid marks (but more on wiping techniques in Chapter 4). If you can drill this into your son's head now, you'll be one step closer to raising a true gentleman—one who will open car doors, say please and thank you, listen attentively, eat with his mouth closed, fart in the bathroom, and most importantly, take care of his mother in her old age.

My Girl Wants to Potty All the Time

Sugar and spice and everything complicated, that's what little girls are made of. When it comes to pee training, girls are, in general, more emotionally mature, more physically mature, and have the added advantage of wearing cute, frilly training pants. But they also come with one special challenge: wiping. Sure, you just place them on the pot, and let it flow, let it flow, let it flow. But unlike boys, you then have to teach their tiny little hands how to dry themselves off. And it ain't no easy feat.

First of all, there's the whole front to back issue. For as you've no doubt been taught by your own mother, you want the motion of the wipe to go from north to south, so that no fecal matter is introduced to the vaginal area: "Nice to meet you, Fecal Matter." "It's a pleasure I'm sure, Vaginal Area." Because the end result of this union could be a nasty and unwanted urinary tract infection.

Next, you'll need to teach your little powder puff how to determine the proper amount of toilet paper to use. Some little girls attempt the one-square-of-tissue wipe, which is in essence, a hand wipe—yuck. Others like to ball up half the roll of toilet paper and leave you with a clogged toilet and another item to put on your endless grocery list. Still others, like my own little princess, can't wipe themselves at all because they've pulled down all the tissue from the roll to watch it form a soft billowy pile on the floor.

Once you do devise a way to teach your girl how to get an accurate method of TP measurement, you then need to teach her the all-important scrunchage of the paper itself. Some sweethearts ball the tissue so tight that it's like wiping themselves with a rock. The paper needs to have the right amount of fluff or that delicate skin can get scraped, and then *ouch*, there goes the potty training altogether. Others don't ball at all, but just run the toilet paper close to the wet area somewhere in between the legs and the water itself, forgoing the wipe all together. What you need to do is explain the "soft touch." They're not scrubbing pots and pans, at least not yet. The bottom line is that wiping is a fragile balance of many factors, all to be refined and mastered over time with lots of practice. Just make sure there's a plunger handy, lots of hand washing, and plenty of bulk-sized packages of toilet paper stored in your garage.

Another wiping concern that comes into play whenever your little passion flower graduates to the big potty (assuming that she didn't start off that way), is that it may be difficult for her to balance herself on top of the toilet with one hand clutching the seat while the other hand pulls off enough toilet paper, scrunches it up, and wipes herself dry. Chances are that she'll need both hands for these tricky tasks, which may result in a fear of falling in. If this is the case, then either get yourself a toilet seat adapter to make her feel more secure, or, if you're at some toilet away from home, have your daughter get off the toilet after she pees, then start the wiping process with her two feet planted solidly on the ground. Sure, she may get a little drizzle drippage that runs down her legs, but keep in mind, urine is sterile. Although it may give you the heebee jeebees seeing pee running down her leg, it won't give her any type of infection. Just give it a quick wipe and all will be fine.

There's one other concern that may come into play when trying to housebreak a female. There are inevitably a few little girls who want to try peeing standing up. After all, she saw Daddy do it, and big brother, and it looked like so much fun. If it happens, don't make a big deal out of it. Explain that girls, even Mommy, need to sit down in order to pee. Let her watch you a few times if she hasn't already (yeah, right). Then, if she still insists on giving it a go, let her go for it. Chances are, the utter discomfort of having warm urine run down her leg, wet shoes and socks, and the ensuing embarrassment (and teasing from big brother) will be enough to curb any more enthusiasm.

If you're feeling overwhelmed or discouraged, let me leave you with this thought: There is nothing cuter in this world than your baby girl sitting on the potty, making tinkle, balling up the toilet paper, and wiping herself. Your heart will grow three sizes at the sight out of pure instinct.

Who knows why? Perhaps it's a just bone Mother Nature throws us to keep up our morale as we head into training for number two.

Holding It In

We all do it. Even grownups do it. Whether we're in line at the bank or trying not to miss the climactic ending of *Desperate Housewives*, we cross our legs and cross our fingers that we can hold it in long enough to get to a bathroom in time. When we finally make it to our destination, we're rewarded by knowing that we've timed it out just right and by that incredibly sweet sensation of peeing when we really, really, really have to go.

That's why we know exactly what's going on when we see our little ones trying to hold it in. With a vice grip on their crotch, they jiggle up and down and do the enormously popular potty dance of the under-five crowd because their tiny tank is full and they're ready to explode. Sure, it drives us crazy. We beg and plead for them to go to the bathroom, but they won't budge. They stand there and lie to us that they don't have to pee as they squeeze their legs together tighter than Donna Martin in *Beverly Hills 90210*.

Like us big people, children can hold it in for any number of different reasons. Let's discuss the most common ones right here and now.

Sheer Terror

For nubile toilet users, fear is a big incentive for doing the tinkle tango. Not fear of the process of peeing, mind you, but fear of the toilet itself. A toilet opens the door to fright and fantasy in a toddler's developing mind. "What if I fall into the hole? Or worse, what if it sucks me down? I'm afraid of the dark, and I can't swim without my floaties!" Keep in mind, you're dealing with a wild child with a young imagination, and nothing invites horror more than a water-filled hole with a dark circle for a drain that leads into the unknown. There could be evil monsters or daddy long-legs down there.

We try to educate our young 'uns by informing them that nothing could ever live down there, but it does no good. Instead of letting you relieve their fears, they just fight you on the subject. Deep down, you know exactly how they feel. I remember when I first saw *Jaws* and how afterwards my heart raced whenever I sat down on the seat, fearing that a salt-water sea creature could somehow make its way up the sewer system and bite me on the ass. If you're younger than I, you no doubt feared snakes because of the film *Anaconda*. And if you're from the Florida area, your ass-biting fear of choice would probably be the crocodile. Ass-biting fear is determined by age and region.

If your child is riddled with fears of the actual toilet, stick with a potty chair—at least for now. In time, the toilet trauma will dissipate. He'll see you, his siblings, and his friends at school using the potty, and eventually, he'll be brave enough to use the big seat with confidence. Or he'll be old enough that his butt will be big enough to completely cover the seat. With age comes wisdom—and a wider ass.

You can also try a potty security object— a doll infused with magic powers to keep your little one safe and secure while on the pot. Just try not to let yourself be the potty security object or you will have no life from this point on. Remember, toddlers pee a bazillion times a day, and we're working on potty independence here.

Once you get your child to sit on the pot and do his business, then there's the whole flushing issue to deal with. Think about it. If you were this tiny little person with tiny little ears, and you had to sit on a huge, cold, ugly

contraption that exploded when you were finished, you would hold it in, too. And heaven
help you if you have one of the water-saving
toilets that sounds like you're blasting off into
outer space every time you push the lever. Worse
still are the automatic toilets at airports or malls
that often don't have the decency to let you stand
up before they detonate.

The bottom line is that a flush noise can be
quite unsettling even for us big folks. Magnify
this a hundred times, and that's how your toddler
feels. If noise is causing your little one to hold
it in, or worse, sabotaging your potty-training
efforts, forgo the flush for the time being. After
he does his business, wait until he's well away
from the bathroom, and then do it yourself. When
he's older and more secure in his toileting abilities, you can go back to the flushing issue. Start
with Junior outside the room, and then gradually
have him move closer and closer to the toilet as
you flush it. Keep the atmosphere light, and be
patient. Let him move at his own pace. You can
also try to incorporate the flushing sound with a
song like "Pop Goes the Weasel," substituting a
flush for the pop. Just be prepared: If this method
works, he'll think of the toilet as a musical instrument and want to "play" it all the time. Sure he'll

get over his flushing fear, but you'll be scared to death when you get your water bill!

Most importantly, do not belittle your child or be angered by his fears. Not only are such reactions just plain mean, they will only serve to grow his fears into a full-blown phobia, and then you'll really be in for it. And for the love of the Wiggles, don't let him watch *Jaws* or any of its 400 sequels until he's well over the voting age.

It Hurts

There are certain medical conditions that can make peeing painful. Urinary tract infections (UTIs), one of the biggies, are caused by several different things, including improper wiping or soap bubbles in the bathwater. In addition to UTIs, your child can also come down with certain rashes or yeast infections that can cause burning and stinging while he pees (as described in Chapter 5). Of course, these conditions are mostly reserved for girls, but you shouldn't rule out a medical reason for pain if your son is complaining when he pees as well. While the motivation to hold it is understandable, doing so, especially when illness is involved, can only make matters worse. When this happens, a call to your pediatrician is in order. These conditions can usually

be treated very quickly, and your kid will be back
on the can in no time.

Laziness

Toddlers lead a very active life. There are bugs
to catch and lint to eat. Their day is really quite
full. That's why most kids don't want to take a
bathroom break. They are having too much fun,
are way too busy, or plain don't want to be both-
ered to stop what they're doing, walk to the bathroom, and take down their pants to pee. The old
way of going in a diaper is so much more convenient than having to exert all of this effort. Gosh,
Mom, this new plan is a total buzz kill.

If you want to train your child to use the
potty, you're going to have to help him pencil in
the time to pee. If your little one is entrenched in
a game of tinker toys, nudge him once in a while
to take a break. If he's deep into an episode of
Blue's Clues and you see him doing the same, step
in so nobody has to sit down in pee.

Keep in mind that what I'm talking about
here are gentle reminders. Remember, nagging
is a no-no—even if it means that your child has
an accident from time to time. Remember that
while your little one is the pilot of his potty-
training ship, you are still his wing man, and as

such, you sometimes need to give your captain some assistance. But not so much that you're forcing the issue. After all, there's the whole power struggle thing that you want to avoid at all costs, which brings me to the most frustrating reason for holding it in.

Parental Control

If your child is "holding it in" as a means of controlling you, in other words, to piss you off, then you have my permission to do the following: Go to your room, put your face in a pillow, and *scream at the top of your lungs.* Then beat said pillow until there is nothing left but feathers and a few strands of cloth. Take a deep breath. Pick the feathers out of your hair. Then return to your child. Chances are that by the time you return, he'll have peed all over himself and is beginning to feel uncomfortable. If there are others present, he is probably being teased unmercifully. Whatever you do, stay calm. What he wants is a reaction from you. Casually change his clothes, tell him calmly that it's too bad he didn't make it to the potty in time, and then drop the subject.

Do this every time the possibility of a power struggle emerges and eventually, your child will get bored when he fails to get a rise out of you.

Toddlers may be willful, but thankfully they have a very short attention span. If they aren't being amused by your temper tantrums, they'll find something more exciting to entertain themselves with, like catching more bugs or eating more lint.

Changing someone's actions without letting them know that you're doing it is a tactic that women have perfected over years. Not only is it good for potty-training struggles, it's what most marriages are based on as well. Remember in *My Big Fat Greek Wedding*, when Toula wanted to go to college but her father didn't want her to? Her mom said, "The man is the head [of the family], but the woman is the neck. And she can turn the head any way she wants." In this case, your child may be the urethra, but you are the genitals, and you can get that urethra to turn any way you want!

If your kid is especially gifted in the stubborn department and this "not letting him see you scream" method doesn't work for you, try this. Tell your child that if he continues to hold it in, he could get an infection and have to go to the doctor. Hopefully, his fear of the doctor will overcome his desire to torment you. I know it sounds cruel, but sometimes you have to be cruel to be clean. And besides, after months of this insanity, you'll think it's the greatest idea since nonfat iced blended mochas.

Potty Proclivities

Let's face it. Kids can be weird about whiz. But when you think about it, why should this aspect of their life be any different from all the others? Chances are you're already dealing with a child who exhibits freakish behavior about most other aspects of his life. Look at clothing choices, for instance: no socks with seams, no clothes with tags, only shirts that have been ironed, only shirts that have not been ironed . . . on and on it goes. I'll bet your child also has a proclivity for strange fashions. Maybe you have a son who will only wear his Superman costume day in and day out. A daughter who refuses to wear anything that's not purple. And what about food issues? No bread with crust, nothing white, food cannot touch another food on the plate, all hot dogs must have the skins peeled off, and may the good Lord help you if you serve up anything green. We've given birth to a society of miniature food critics with a constantly changing palate.

“ My daughter went through a phase when she refused to wear any underwear. I thought it best to let her outgrow this phase on her own but then had to intervene when she learned how to hang upside down on the bar at the park. ”

—Amelia

Yes, proclivities are ingrained in the hard wiring of a toddler's brain. We all know at least one who won't go to birthday parties that have live characters, who won't walk on wet grass, and who refuse to touch sand. But in no place are kids stranger than they are when dealing with the potty. This is where proclivities can bloom to full flower. After all, we parents are so desperate to have our offspring's derriere dry that we'll let them do just about anything they want in order to attain our goal. There are the outdoorsmen toddlers: the ones who will only pee in the back yard and mark their territory like dogs. Hey, at least they're out of diapers, and getting a little fresh air while they're at it. Besides, if you lived in the woods of the Appalachians instead of in an apartment with a shared courtyard, this wouldn't be an issue at all.

Then there are the ones (mostly boys) who want to use absolutely every public restroom they can locate. If his little guy is within four walls that contain plumbing, he wants to use the potty. And who are you to argue? You don't want to say no. I mean, what if it's a real emergency? Besides, he does manage to squeeze out a little something each and every time.

Then there are the wiping proclivities: They'll only use white toilet paper, or worse, the pink quilted kind that's been discontinued. Or there are the ones who are particular about softness. And what about the kids who will only wear one certain kind of disposable training pants that has a specific Disney character on them that they only sell in the summer months and at only one particular store in Florida that you now have to special order because you were stupid enough to indulge this proclivity on your two-week vacation to Disney World last summer and now it's grown into a full-grown obsession? Whew. I'm exhausted just writing about it.

Probably the most common pee proclivity of all is the inability to pee away from home. You've got your poor kid so conditioned to using his potty-chair or toilet at home that he can't go far without it. As you can imagine, this can lead to big problems if you ever have to leave the house, go on vacation, or (worst-case scenario) have Thanksgiving dinner at your in-laws'. Good, bad, or indifferent, kids can hold in their poops for days, like a camel holds water, but pee is another issue entirely.

If your kid is a potty phobic, there are a few things you can try:

- Put diapers on your child when you're away from home. I know this goes against everything you've been working toward so far, but your child's resistance to foreign potties could indicate he's not completely ready to be potty trained. After all, Rome probably wasn't even built in a few months.

- Bring your home potty chair with you everywhere you go. They are portable, and I've heard that people actually do this. If your child uses the toilet seat adaptor, get the kind that folds up for easier packing.

- Travel with paper cups. My friend had to travel with her stubborn daughter who refused to put her tush on anything other than her home toilet. Whenever they were away from home, she had her stand in the bathroom stall with her legs slightly apart, and put a cup underneath her to catch the pee. I know it sounds indulgent and maybe even whacky, but she said it was a heck of a lot easier than having people watch her while the kid took a leak at an O'Hare boarding area while waiting for a connecting flight.

Your best option when dealing with a potty phobia is probably behind door number four: Work through it. Your child needs to, at some point in his life, learn to take a leak away from home. Do not get annoyed or frustrated, for as I've told you a million times before, it can only make matters worse. After all, you've got neurosis in the making here. You want to discourage it, not feed it chocolate and strawberries. You'll find that if you can get your kid to use the potty away from home just one time, there's a good chance that the spell will be broken and the phobia will end.

Don't Get Pissed Off

I know I keep hinting around the issue—okay, beating you over the head with it—so let's just take a minute to actually talk about it. Your temper. Are you being pushed to the limit? Are you able to control it, or do you constantly have to count to ten? Do pee stains on the rug send steam shooting out of your ears and make you want to trade in your child for a pair of Jimmy Choos? What you need to know is that right now, your kid has you over a barrel. Chances are that he knows it, too. Your child can and will take full advantage of the fact that he is in the driver's seat. If this is true for you, you must stop right here. You have to get the keys back before he steers you over a cliff. And the only way to do this is to remain calm. If you get mad, you give away your power, and you officially set yourself up for the ugliest, if not the stinkiest, game of cat-and-mouse known to man.

We all know that toddlers are notoriously contrasuggestive. They have no choice. It's a physiological mechanism that lasts from approximately age two to age four, and then tends to resurface again during the turbulent teenage years. Potty training is no different from any other battle that you'll have to fight with these mini-demons, be it "Please put on that shirt," to "Please eat your peas," to "Please give Mommy the remote control that you're dangling over the fishbowl." You expect your little one to willingly go along with this recent endeavor, which essentially means more work for him? You're crazy.

The more you show that you really want your child to give up his diapers, the more he's going to fight you on the idea. The more you beg him to make tinkle and poo-poo in the potty, the longer he'll hold it. After all, it's his body. And while you may be bigger, louder, and completely in charge of everything else in Junior's universe, his eliminations fall solely in his jurisdiction. Woo hoo! Imagine how powerful that makes him feel after years of oppression.

He'll tease you and taunt you. He'll feign interest in the potty. He'll even placate you with a few turds and tinkles in the bowl. You'll throw a party, call everyone you know, and be happy for the first time in months. But then he'll pull a bait and switch, losing all interest in the potty and reverting to his diaper-wearing ways. Then, just like that, it's over. Exactly like that guy in high school who pursued you diligently, then, when you finally reciprocated his affections, dumped you like a rotten Brussels sprout. The potty chair sits in the corner collecting spider webs, and you're left alone on prom night with a broken heart.

If the aggravation doesn't get to you, the tedium will. He'll sit on the pot so long that a ring will be permanently indented on his ass, with nothing in the can to show for it. And all the while he'll demand that you sit beside him, read him a story, sing him a song, and feed him a handful of grapes while a bevy of costume characters perform Raffi's greatest hits. And you do it. You do it all. You perform the "run the faucet" trick, the "finger tipping in the bowl of warm water" stunt, and even play the new white-noise machine you got from Sharper Image on the waterfall setting. Alas, your kid remains as dry as the Sahara (although you've peed about fifty-five times).

The greatest test of your temper will come from your kid's smarts—and some little tykes have these in excess. There's the one little devil that pours apple juice into the bowl so that his mommy will think that he's peed and reward him with a few colorful M&M's. Or the one who shows Mommy the recently flushed toilet and swear that he's just made a pee-pee in it. Great, honey. Have some M&M's. And we must not forget the one who has built up his pee-pee muscles so well that he's able to squeeze out a few drops of pee every twenty minutes. Give me my bulk-size bag of M&M's now, thank you very much.

Whatever you do, don't underestimate the intelligence of a toddler going through toileting. So maybe he can't count to ten, and sure, he continues to lick the end of a battery even though it shocks him, but that doesn't make him stupid. He most likely has the brainpower of a criminal mastermind. He knows exactly how to play you to get your undivided attention and make you sit on the cold bathroom floor to boot. He can pee on cue when he's got a hankering for some Skittles. And he knows that he can unwind an entire roll of toilet paper onto the floor without repercussions if he rewards you with some pee in the bowl when he's through.

The bottom line is that potty training is like giving your kid a magical pass into the greatest kingdom in the world. It's your job to not let him use this pass. If you do, you'll be manipulated, frustrated, and controlled. You don't have to sit on the bathroom floor for hours while Junior sits on the throne. You can haul in a comfy chair, and let Junior read his own potty books while you kick back and enjoy some tabloid magazines. Or better yet, leave Junior alone with a copy of your *People* magazine (hey, it's helped million of people poop for decades) and use the time to answer some e-mails.

Keep in mind that potty training is not the appropriate venue for punishment. It serves no purpose except to let you vent your anger and frustrations, and that's what husbands are for. Your child is in a developmental stage that he is in no way capable of comprehending. Doctors and therapists spend entire careers analyzing the potty-training process and its ramifications in the development of the human psyche. (Have they nothing better to do?) There are so many synapses firing off in that little toddler brain that it's like one big cerebral Fourth of July in there. Yelling at him for not performing according to plan is like raining on his parade and dousing out all the sparkly colored lights.

Remember, it's love that's the battlefield, not potty training. And if you're finding yourself in a constant state of irritation, you must ask yourself if maybe it's not the right time to jump this hurdle. Maybe your child isn't ready. Maybe you aren't ready. Maybe a break from this whole shebang is in order. Maybe not. Just know that your child will be potty trained one day, so don't destroy your future relationship on account of it. After all, this is the apple of your eye we're talking about.

Keep things in perspective. Don't be taken advantage of, and for heaven's sake, keep calm. If potty training is anything, it's a delicate balance of keeping your child entertained and encouraged while maintaining your own dignity. Remember, toddlers just want to have fun. As soon as there's pressure to produce, and toddler doesn't see it as a party anymore, potty training will take an abrupt turn for the ugly. So take the pressure off, take a step back, and just . . . go with the flow!

Chapter 4

the scoop on poop

Many of the books and so-called experts on potty training tell you that your child will learn to poop in the potty long before she learns to pee. But my own unofficial, unscientific, and completely unproven poll of real experts (a.k.a. my friends and other actual mommies) indicates that poop training follows pee training approximately 99.9 percent of the time. (Actually, it was 100 percent, but I have to leave a little wiggle room so I won't get sued for passing on false data.) Poop smarts can be a far greater challenge to learn, for various reasons.

It's true that your little pooping machine has an easier time recognizing the sensation of needing to have a bowel movement, so that part's a cinch. You may also have the added benefit of knowing when your toddler has to go poop because their bowels tend to have Swiss-timing accuracy. For these reasons, you'd think that poo training would be easy-peasy, light and breezy. But think again. There are still plenty of hurdles to overcome when trying to get Junior to move those bowels into the potty. In fact, going number one is a cakewalk compared with going number two. And if you're like most of us real moms, you'll find yourself fighting for poop training long after tinkle training is achieved.

Why is this? It's anyone's guess. It could be because kids only poop once or twice a day, so they don't get the same practice time that they do with tinkles. Problems could also stem from the complex act of wiping that, let's face it, can be overlooked with pee without much fanfare. Immaturity, emotional issues, control, fear, or just plain laziness can also cause the poo-poo lag. But probably the number-one reason for the number-two difficulty is that poop is simply harder to deal with. It stinks, it smears, it stains—it's (dare I say) just plain *shitty*.

"They" tell you that you shouldn't show disgust at your child's feces for fear that it might hurt your wee one's feelings. After all, the stinky poop that makes your eyes water and burns the hair in your nostrils just came out of your little pride and joy. And if you respond to it negatively, "they" feel that it could send a negative message to your child and affect her self-esteem. While I understand this on an intellectual level, we mommies live on a practical level, and it's really hard to do in real life. Yes, you love your child unconditionally, but isn't there some loophole that says you don't have to love all of her bodily functions, in particular the Olympic gold-medal winning doo-doo that just filled her diaper and leaked all the way up to her neck?

"They" also say that boys can be much more difficult to train and take far longer to learn than girls. But why, you frantic mothers of boys might ask? Perhaps it is the emotional immaturity of boys. Perhaps their bowels and intestinal systems develop more slowly. Control is one of the major issues. Because of this, some boys can take years to train. If you're lucky, poop training won't be a huge ordeal, and he'll take to it as naturally as he does holding onto his penis as he falls to sleep.

Regardless of this minor setback, let's face it—in the long run, the boys are far more successful in the BM arena. Think of your husband, your brothers and boyfriends, even your father, any of whom could sit on the toilet and freaking poop all day! We females fight constipation from the moment we get our first training bra and fear pooping anywhere but in the privacy of our own comforting toilets. Males, on the other hand, think of each "movement" as a spa day and spend long, leisurely, luxurious hours on the can getting caught up on reading. And without shame yet! What man hesitates to grab the sports section, take a seat in a public restroom (which, by the way, is alongside ten other stalls), and cut loose with his version of the song of the trumpeting swan?

Whether poop training comes before or after learning how to pee in the pot and whether it takes longer for boys to conquer than girls are things that only time will tell. But it is going to happen at some point in the lives of your little ones. So before it does, let me fill you in on all the poop there is to know about . . . well . . . about poop.

The Poop Hold

You've been trying to potty train your kid for what feels like years now. She's been successfully making tinkle in the potty for weeks, but she has refused to take off her diaper for the big jobs. Then, three days ago, at exactly 8:07 a.m., precisely twelve minutes after she finished eating her bowl of Cap 'N Crunch, the heavens parted. She said she had to make poopie, and you marched her into the bathroom, placed her on the potty, and right on cue, she pooped! You jumped for joy and smiled with glee. There were stickers, stars, and a small marching band. Your mission was accomplished. You hadn't been this happy since you fit into your pre-pregnancy jeans (okay, your pre-pregnancy fat jeans). You can now die a happy, happy woman!

For many of you, this will mark the official end of your potty-training trek. Now that your child has overcome her fears and other issues in the poop department, your job is done. But for others—for *most* others—this may not be the end. In fact, it may only be the middle. For now you may embark on the all-too-common "holding it in" phase, an issue that can stay with your child for years to come. And while holding it in with pee results in wet clothing and spots on rugs, holding it in with poop can result in much more serious consequences.

There are many reasons why children hold onto their poop as if it were the secret recipe for Colonel Sanders's eleven famous herbs and spices. Here are some of the most common reasons why your kid might keep his anus closed for business.

The Psychology of Poo

It seems that toddlers have two entirely different belief systems when it comes to excrement. Pee is seen as "excrement lite," and it harbors no deep-seated meaning for toddlers. But poo can be hard core, both figuratively and literally. (More about that on page 116, when we get to chat about constipation.) Toddlers attach so much psychological significance to their poop that each dump is like its own Rorschach test. On some strange level, your little one sees her turd as an extension of herself, sort of like another body part like an arm or a leg. While it's nothing to you, seeing that piece of herself flushed down the toilet can be very traumatic to your child. If this is the situation you're going through, don't flush the toilet after she's finished. Just walk away and give it a flush as soon as you can distract her. Just don't get *too* distracted. If you forget to flush, your kid may come back into the bathroom, fish it out, and use it as a source of modeling clay (more on that later on as well).

Also, if your trainee is on the younger side or less emotionally mature, she may be holding in her poops out of sheer possessiveness. Toddlers are not famous for their ability to share, and to them, poop is no different from a favorite dolly or action figure. They are seriously reluctant to give it up, and what better place to store it than inside of their tummies, where you can't get to it?

Fear of Big Poops

Besides your average, run-of-the-mill potty fears like flush sounds, sewer sharks, snakes, and crocs, there is also the fear of passing large, hard stools. Understandably, after going through this experience even once, the very thought of this can scare the bejeebers out of any tiny tuckus. As we know, poops come in many shapes and sizes. We also know that the size of the container (namely, your child) is in no way indicative of the size of what comes out of it (namely, her poop). You will find that what emerges from your child often appears to be larger than your child herself. It's one of those unfathomable things, like how a TV works or why your washer breaks down just days after the warrantee expires.

It can be quite a scary experience if your little one makes a grande-, or worse, a vente-sized poop. On top of this, if the stool is the least bit hard, it can most assuredly hurt. And once this happens, you'll find that you're in deep doo-doo. Now that your child associates poop-ing with pain, she is likely to begin holding it in. This may result in constipation and harder stools, thereby leading to even more pain and setting off the vicious cycle that can spin you into insanity. If you're in the midst of this cycle, it's going to take some serious support and cajol-ing, along with some other useful tips, to get the factory up and running again (see "Much Ado about Poo" on page 116). If this doesn't work, call your pediatrician. He may suggest mineral oil or, in some heavy-duty cases, laxatives. Please don't try either of these solutions except on your pediatrician's advice.

The one and only benefit of these super-sized turds is that they will teach you to become quite the knowledgeable plumber. For your kid's mambo jambos will keep your toilets constantly clogged. My biggest piece of advice for these big pieces it to keep a plunger handy next to every toilet bowl in the house. Before you begin poo training, you should also learn how to quickly turn off the water so you can keep your bathroom floor from looking like a sewage waste facility. (See "My Toilet Runneth Over," in Chapter 6.)

Stress

Just as with grownups, stress can make children hold in their BMs. It's not necessarily a conscious choice but rather has something to do with tension causing the sphincter muscles to constrict. Any major toddler issue like a new sibling, new babysitter or new sheets can cause a toddler to feel pressure, and therefore might trigger this unconscious control issue.

Traveler's Constipation

And speaking of what we big folks can relate to, how about pooping away from home? Frankly, I'm right there with the little tots on this one and find it to be an excellent reason for holding it in. Still, it's not really the best situation to deal with—especially if your child is in day care, at Grandma's, or with you on vacation. Traveler's constipation could also become a real issue for those of you who share custody. Your child's colon may run free all week, but once she returns from a weekend at her father's she's cantankerous, crabby, and crammed up with crap.

Control

By far the most frustrating reason that a toddler controls her goods is as a conscious means of controlling you. As you know, it's easier to hold in poop than pee, and once your little dickens sets her mind to it, she can hold it in for *days*. It's as if she's equipped with a sphincter infused with superhero strength. All human toddlers have this special gift. They're born with it. Unfortunately, it wears off as we age, along with dewy fresh cheeks. By the time we're elderly, it may even cease to function altogether. Sad but true. This issue of control will absolutely be the biggest issue that you and your child will ever face—that is, until your toddler becomes a teenager and wants to drop out of high school and join a band.

What generally happens is that parents, in their push to get their kids poop trained, make the massive mistake of giving the kids the message that this is something that they really, really want them to do. Of course, the little one then sees this as *way* too much parental domination, and being the little control freak that she is, decides to put Mommy and Daddy in their place.

Next comes a sort of "emotional constipation" that can lead to the crumbling of life as you now know it. Your child holds it in. The stools get harder and larger. Eventually, your little one not only loses her desire to poop but her ability to contain her poop. There are explosions and leaks, and you're left weeping in the laundry room while you pretreat every article of clothing your child wears on her bottom half.

The best way to avoid control issues with your child is to stay calm about poo training. Don't let your kid see your cards and know how happy she makes you when she uses the toilet. You may be bigger, but your kid's rectum is stronger, and you're never going to win this battle in a healthy way. Therefore, it's best to stop fighting at all.

If you're in deep, put a diaper on your kid and call it a day. Take a moment to regroup and re-energize. When you feel strong, try again. But be sure to pick a good time to start up. Make sure it's a time when your child isn't in a negative phase, under any stress, suffering from any fears, or being forced to try a new food group. Most importantly, be sure that she's in a "new poo state

> **❝** My son once held in his poop for eight days. I could only imagine that his digestive system was so full that soon he'd be pooping when he coughed. **❞**
>
> —Kelly

of mind." In other words, let enough time pass for her to forget how important this is for you, so that you can have the upper hand. Until that time, you're inviting disaster, and you'll not only be dealing with a toddler who holds it in, but the repercussions that will follow. Which is the perfect segue into this next section.

Much Ado about Poo (a.k.a. Constipation)

Note: The following section contains graphic details of defecation and is not intended for the weak of heart or for anyone unable to laugh at grade-school humor.

If, for whatever reason, your child has become possessive of her precious poops, then what started off as merely a bad situation could quite possibly progress to an all-out ugly state of affairs. On top of feeling out of control and under pressure to learn to poop in a pot, and besides feeling ornery from having a colon full of crap, there's an excellent chance that your child will also become constipated.

If this happens, you can get ready to experience the darkest days of the whole potty-training experience. When you look back upon these times years from now, your eyes will well up with tears and your body will tremble in fear. For when a child contains her BMs in her body, a snowball effect occurs deep within her colon. Her stool keeps growing and growing, creating a giant "snowturd." Not only does this snowturd become huge, but it also becomes as hard as a bad boob job. The longer it's held inside, the bigger and drier it becomes, until your precious toddler has boulder-sized snowturds stacked up inside her teeny-tiny tummy. Then, when her body can hold it no more, she's forced to squeeze those giant turds out through a hole the width of a number-two pencil. Anyone who's been through labor knows exactly how scary that ordeal sounds.

If your child suspects that pooping is gonna hurt, she ain't gonna poop. And thus begins the vicious cycle of holding it in, thereby producing harder and larger stools. If the problem is left unchecked for too long, the only way to unclog those backed-up pipes is with a can of full-strength prune juice and a plumber's snake.

Sometimes stools become so large that they stretch the toddler's rectum, making it difficult for her to recognize the sensation of having to poop. The body continues to manufacture feces, which builds up to the point that it actually leaks out of the anus. In poop-ese, this is called encopresis. Parents might think that their child is pooping in her pants all day long, when in reality her tiny rectum is unable to contain the massive amount of waste pressing down on it. What appears to be diarrhea is actually chronic constipation. Not only is this disconcerting to the parents, who so desperately want the poops in the pot, it can be embarrassing and demeaning to your child, who will now be referred to as "Little Miss Stinky Pants" until long after high school graduation.

Worse, the straining involved in passing Mount Poopmore can cause tiny cracks or tears around the rectum. These are called fissures. If there is blood around your child's stools, and she screams in agony whenever she poops, there's a good chance that the blood and pain are being caused by a fissure. Call your pediatrician immediately. Fissures are not life threatening, but oy vey, do they hurt. Just think about it . . . okay, don't. But as you can see, it's important to try your ding-dong hardest to never *ever* let your kid get constipated.

If you suspect that your kid is clogged up, you should deal with it as soon as possible, before your child is forced to give birth to these snowturds. Fortunately, the signs of a constipated toddler are rather easy to spot. Ask yourself these questions:

- Have her bowel movements ceased to exist, or become few and far between?
- Are the poops small, hard, and dry? Or huge, hard, and dry?
- Are your child's bowel movements painful?
- Is your child crabby, cranky, and uncomfortable?
- Is your child doing the poo-poo dance? (This is a wiggly jig that's usually combined with an arched back and a butt that's sticking straight out behind her.)
- Have you been trying to poop train your child by nagging, pressuring, or drawing too much attention to the training process?

If you answered yes to two or more of the above questions, then you've got the makings for the big "C."

Don't get me wrong; many other things can cause constipation besides just a willful potty trainee. Constipation can go hand-in-hand with certain illnesses, medications, and stress. But probably the number-one cause of uninvited constipation in children is (drum roll, please) the basic poor diet. Fortunately, that's something that you can control. If you want to poop train your kid, make sure that you feed her a balanced diet with plenty of fiber. This will help keep the plumbing as clear as Route 66 at three in the morning.

If Junior is already constipated, you should speak with your doctor. He or she may suggest that you give your child a little mineral oil or other over-the-counter medication. But please, never, never, *never* give your child laxatives, suppositories, or enemas without a doctor's advice. (If you do, I will personally come over to your house and hit you upside your head.) Better plan, try the following steps to loosen things up and get the potty train back on track:

- Along with lots of sunshine, and plenty of love, children need a healthy diet to thrive and go poop. We're talking whole-wheat, whole-grain products, lots of veggies, fresh fruit, dried fruit, which of course includes everybody's favorite poop-producer, prunes. It's also best to steer clear of those yummy, yet potentially constipating pieces of cheese that Junior gobbles up like candy.

- Give your kid plenty of water. And I do mean water. Not juice boxes or milk or any of that neon blue or green liquid that looks like it comes from outer space. Water keeps those poops soft and supple. Simply stated, the more water that goes in, the easier the poop comes out.

- If you want the bowels moving, you need to get the body moving, too. As always, make sure that your child gets plenty of exercise.

- Lube it up. If painful stools are holding Junior back, put a little Vaseline around the anus to help slide 'em through.

- When it's bath time, have your clogged kid soak in a warm bath with her legs crossed so that a bit of water can get in and loosen things up a bit.

Make sure to tell your child that these steps will make the hard and painful poo-poos go away. And while you're at it, try the above tips in your own life as well—eat healthy, drink plenty of fluids, and exercise. (You don't have to cross your legs in the bathtub unless it's something you feel you want to try.) Yes, I know, we've all heard it a million times. But that's because there's something to it. Remember, you are the role model for your child. If you survive on junk food and TV, so will she. If you want to combat and prevent constipation in your child, take care of yourself, and your little one will follow. By doing so, you'll say good-bye to those nasty snowturds and you'll have the healthiest bowels on the block.

Wipe Out

It's not easy being three. Not only do you have to remember to say "please" and "thank you" and "I'm sorry that I flushed your engagement ring down the toilet during my last tantrum," you also have to master the difficult task of wiping your butt after you poop. And this task can make learning your ABCs seem like child's play. Yes, a young child must learn the Cirque de Soleil maneuver of balancing herself on the pot while tearing off the proper amount of toilet paper to clean but not clog, and twist her torso around to wipe an area that she can't even see.

What's a toddler to do? Better yet, what's a toddler's mom to do? To begin with, realize that it's going to take some time. A lot of young kiddies just aren't equipped to wipe themselves yet.

Maybe they haven't developed the dexterity to accomplish such a task, or maybe they're just not emotionally ready to release Mommy from her bathroom duties. In the midst of these frustrating times, you may find yourself wondering, "What the heck was the problem with diapers anyway?" After all, with diapers the wiping wasn't fun, but at least it was doo-doo able. Everything was spread out before you like the *New York Times* on Sunday morning. Now, getting your kid's ass clean is like getting tomato-sauce stains off your Tupperware: impossible!

When wiping your young one's derriere, the challenge is that her butt is either sitting down on a potty where you can't get to it, or standing up where her butt cheeks are clenched tighter than Joan River's face. You have to do some fancy moves to get to the goods. If your kid likes to sit down to be wiped, have her lean forward. If your child prefers to stand, have her bend over. This should crack open the case wide enough so you can get to the poo without problem. This task of wiping your kid's rump after she takes a dump can go on for some time, and like anything else, practice does indeed make perfect.

Here's a word of caution: Make sure that you wipe your kid as well as you would with a diaper

66 My daughter was so afraid to use the big toilet because she thought she'd fall in. After weeks of promising her that she wouldn't, she climbed on top and did her business. But then she let go of the seat to tear off some paper, and her tush fell right into the water! She screamed and screamed and months later, I still can't get her to try it again. 99

—Laurie

change. If your kid's butt doesn't shine, she is still prone to getting a rash. Hours after an ineffective poo-poo wipe, she'll be scratching herself as if you wiped her with poison ivy. It's also important to wash your hands after you wipe and to have your kid do it. Not only is it the sanitary thing to do, but monkey see, monkey doo-doo.

What about the kid who absolutely refuses to let you wipe her and insists on doing it herself? This isn't such a problem if you've given birth to the Queen of Clean, but it's a huge issue if your kid's butt cheeks end up looking like a dog park when she's through.

There are several reasons your child may push away your helping hand. Perhaps she doesn't want you touching her masterpiece. Perhaps the whole wiping process has become too personal to her.

Or maybe she's just plain afraid. After all, the last time you wiped her, you wiped her clear off the toilet (don't worry, you weren't the only one).

So what's the answer? Well, we all know how toddlers can be. Is it really worth staging a Battle of the Network Stars to get her tushie clean enough to eat off of? How clean is clean? Is there a standard of butt cleanliness? A chart that we can refer to compare our child's ass cheeks? And are your standards too high? After all, it *is* only a tushie. No one's going to see it under clothing or do a "white glove test" to check for debris, and a little rash won't cause any permanent harm.

This is what I think: You've just fought for months to finally get Junior to poop in the potty, and you've won that battle. Starting a brand-new one now over wiping dominance is like inviting Donald Trump and Rosie O'Donnell into your bathroom. Your child could very well decide to start holding in those poops again over a few squares of TP. Let it go, sister. It's just not worth it.

Now if there are beads of sweat dripping down your brow, and you are quivering with anxiety over the thought of having a bit of fecal debris on your child (and when you put it that way, who wouldn't?), I have two pieces of advice for you. One, schedule bath time immediately following poop time. Two, buy thyself some toddler wipes. Check the shelves of your local supermarket and drugstore for this wonderful new invention. They're basically diaper wipes, but smaller, and they come in a convenient canister that keeps them moist. Your kid can pop one up and wipe her own tuckus all by her wee wittle self. I suggest that you keep a six-pack of these things handy in every bathroom in the house.

There also could be a compromise. In our house, the ideal wiping scenario is akin to the way we do tooth brushing. My daughter does the heavy lifting first, then Mommy comes in at the end for the final cleanup. It seems to satisfy the I-can-do-it-by-myself aspect of a willful toddler along with the but-not-as-good-as-Mommy-can part of a neurotic parent. Thus far, we've got healthy teeth and not one skid mark to speak of.

If your child insists on doing it all by herself, your best plan of attack is to teach her the correct way:

1. Little girls must wipe from front to back after going number two.

2. Practice on a plastic doll, or a GI Joe, or whatever your kid is into. Put a little peanut butter on the tushie and let your toddler wipe it until all the peanut butter is gone.

3. Promote the "soft touch." Aggressive wiping can scratch and damage sensitive skin. If this happens, ouch! Plus, you've got a toddler who's afraid to go potty.

4. If your kid is prone to really big jobs, teach him the mid-poo flush. If your kid is prone to really big wipes, teach him the mid-wipe flush. This is especially helpful when you're away from the comforts of your own home plunger.

5. Try to instruct your child to use a reasonable amount of toilet paper. After all, we must think of the environment, as well as your pipes. But good luck. Unrolling that paper spool is more fun than a day at Chuck E. Cheese.

I know that right now it's quite a physical and emotional experience keeping your kid's ass clean after a poop. Trust me, there will come a day when the behind-cleaning days are behind you.

Potty Poopers

As I mentioned before, poop training can be the biggest challenge of the whole potty-training milieu. Not only is it disgusting to deal so intimately with feces, but kids can be quite picky about how they go about doing their poops. There are those who go to the bathroom only to end up pooping on the floor right next to the potty. There are those who refuse to poop in the house and insist on taking a dump in the back yard along with the birds and butterflies. There are those who insist on being totally naked when they go. There are those, like my daughter, who insist on pooping standing up (at least I hope there are others like her or she's no doubt destined for the Funny Farm). And then there are the ones who test us to the limit: the little Vincent van Poos.

The little poo artist uses his doo-doo as a medium to create lovely sculptures and murals. The experts say that if this happens, you shouldn't make a big deal out of it. They say you should just calmly clean your child up and tell her that "Poo-poo stays in the potty." Then walk her into another room and give her some crayons and paper to create with. That would be fine advice if these experts provided the service of coming over and cleaning up your stinky house! For heaven's sake, we moms are only human. And staying calm when you've got excrement all over your new Laura Ashley wallpaper is pushing it to the limit. Nevertheless, as with everything else in raising a toddler, it probably won't do a bit of good to pop your cork—unless that cork comes out of the bottle of champagne that you guzzle from your rubber-gloved hand while you scrub your walls clean.

Just as wearisome are the kids who are trained to go number one but refuse to go number two in anything but a diaper. They're old enough to recognize the sensation, but still they come to you, diaper in hand no less, and ask you to put them in the darn thing. So you do as they ask for fear of causing yet another tantrum, and they trot off for privacy like a dog with a new bone. After a bit, they return to you for cleanup detail and you comply, rationalizing that your child just isn't ready yet. (We women are master rationalizers, which is why we own so many darn pairs of shoes.)

If this situation sounds familiar, my guess is that you're completely frustrated and at the end of your potty-training rope. This process is taking way too long, and frankly, it's just plain gross. You're sick of planning your day around your child's bowel movements, sick of buying super-sized diapers that could fit a grown person, sick of trying to stuff them inside the bleeping Diaper Genie, and sick of the resentment that you have toward your child (it's okay, we've all been there). Gosh darn dag-nabbit, you're mad as hell, and you're not going to change that diaper anymore!

Hang in there. This irritation can be used for good instead of evil. In fact, it just may be the key to unlocking the hell you now call your life. If what's going on in your personal poop war is purely a battle of wills (and not illness, immaturity, or any other reasonable excuse), it's your complete and total annoyance at the situation that just may motivate you to put an end to the madness. After all, your child was weaned off the breast when *you* were ready. Most likely, she started sleeping through the night when *you* stopped running into her room every time she whimpered or cooed. So after all these months of tiptoeing around potty training and bowing to your child's every whim and wish, maybe now you finally have the inner strength to just say, "No."

If this is the situation that you're in, and your personal thermometer has reached the hard candy stage, try some of the following tactics the next time Junior comes a-callin' for a diaper. They ultimately may not work to poo train your child, but the minor retribution will at least make you feel a little better in the meantime:

1. Tell your child that there are no more diapers.
2. Tell your child to go ahead and poop in her pants or on the floor if she won't use the potty.
3. Tell your child that if she goes anywhere but the toilet, she's the one who's going to clean it up.
4. Put your child outside to poop along with the dogs.

Heinie Hygiene

Yes, I know that we've talked quite a bit about the subject of hygiene, but when dealing with poo-poo, I feel that I must touch on it a bit more. Or rather, not touch it, given that the anus is a virtual wasteland of harmful bacteria and thus a favorite stomping ground for the five-and-under crowd. As we all know, kids love to explore, and their own bodies are one of their favorite places to have an expedition. I'm all for educating children about their bodies and teaching them that there's nothing shameful about any part. But the anus is one body part that should be kept "hands off." If there is any contact between the anus and the child's fingers, the fingers should be scrubbed down like Meryl Streep in *Silkwood*.

Sure, there are other important times to wash your kid's hands as well, like before she eats and if she cuts her finger. But washing up after your child wipes her tuckus is one of the best ways to prevent her from getting sick. Human feces is riddled with dangerous bacteria. When you consider that toddlers constantly like to put things in their mouths, you see that you have a very dangerous combination.

Simply stated, good hygiene should be part and parcel of the whole potty-training experience. Yes, we can only hope that you impart all aspects of good potty manners to your child, including waiting her turn in the potty line, putting the seat down when he's through pishing, wiping any tinkle drops that land on the seat, using a reasonable amount of toilet paper, flushing the toilet when she's done, and, when in a public restroom, resisting the temptation to peek under the next stall to see what's going on over there. But much more importantly, you must teach Junior the skill of washing his hands after using the toilet. If every time you use the bathroom you wash your own filthy hands, and each and every time you train your little one you both wash your hands together, then you're instilling good hygiene habits that will last a lifetime. Not only that, but you'll be preventing numerous illnesses that would warrant your child staying home on a school day (that should be enough motivation right there!)

Teaching your child what to do after using a potty is at least as important, if not more, than what to do while using a potty. Make sure that your child uses water, warm if possible, and plenty of soap. She should rub that soap all around her hands for the time it takes to sing "Row, Row, Row Your Boat," paying close attention to her fingertips. When she's done, make sure that she rinses well and turns off the faucet (not to prevent germs, but to prevent high energy bills and keep from wasting a precious resource).

The drying aspect of the wash experience is basically a bonus, as most toddlers are out the door halfway through the rinse cycle. If drying happens, great. If not, at least you've got the hands somewhat clean, or at least wet and sudsy. If soap is not available, an enthusiastic rub under the water is better than nothing at all. If none of the above is available, use antibacterial lotion with the same top-and-bottom rub, with a flapping of the hands to dry the residual chemicals. As a nice extra, the antibacterial stuff comes in all sorts of fabulous and enticing colors and flavors. Just don't let your child eat it.

Remember, good hygiene is the cherry on your potty-training sundae. The mustache on your poop-training Dr. Phil. And if I can prevent just one preschooler from getting infected with E. coli, then my job is done. Although I guess it really isn't since I have quite a few potty-training things left to tell you about.

66 I spent the weekend visiting my parents, along with all three of my potty-training nieces and nephews. Between their rushed wiping techniques and their not-quite-clean hands, I came home with such a bad bacterial infection that I had trouble getting to the potty in time and had a few accidents of my own. 99

—Susan

accidents happen . . . again and again and again

Let's face it, poo-poo and pee-pee happen. And they happen in places where they should not. In Grandma's lap. In new upholstered furniture. In bank lines. And, after months of struggle, you're sick and tired of it happening at all. Here you thought that after countless talks and visuals, your kid had finally grasped the complex idea that excrement goes inside of the toilet. But your dreams are shattered when, once again, your kid takes a dump in the frozen-food section of the Piggly Wiggly.

I know you're stressed out, but I'm also sure
that you've had years of dealing with disappoint-
ment. Just think back to when you were a little
girl, and you had a vision of what your life would
be like when you grew up. Like most idealis-
tic young princesses raised on post women's-lib
fairy tales and politically correct Barbie dolls,
you had a plan: You'd grow up, go to college,
and meet the man of your dreams. He'd propose
to you on a beach at sunset during your senior
year, and the two of you would marry the first
summer after your first year of graduate school.
It would be the world's most beautiful wedding,
second only to Princess Diana's, with 265 guests
and a full chamber orchestra. You'd wear Grandmother Lilly's wedding dress and a tiara from
Harry Winston, because your gorgeous groom
would have nothing less for you. You'd honeymoon in Bora Bora, then return to your beautiful
five-plus-three home on two acres in upstate New
York. You'd work as a child advocacy attorney,
and he'd be—of course—a veterinarian.

Exactly 3.3 years into wedded bliss, you'd
welcome a baby girl, Rebecca. She'd have blonde
hair, blue eyes, and sleep through the night at
two weeks old. She'd nurse perfectly for one year-
and at six months old, you'd introduce solids,

of course all organic and prepared lovingly from scratch by you. After all, you wouldn't need a nanny. You'd still continue your law practice but part time and from home, working at night and during baby naps, which, by the way, she'd do exactly on schedule. And, of course, with the help of a baby jogger, and your understanding husband who'd insist on babysitting little Becca so you could go to the gym, you'd have your pre-pregnancy figure back in no time flat.

Then, at two and a half, you'd start the potty-training process. She, being a brilliant and compliant wonder, would take to it like a bee to the flower, thus completing your one last commitment to infancy, and freeing you to pursue your dream of becoming the youngest sitting justice on the U.S. Supreme Court.

Hold on a sec, would ya? I'm laughing so hard, I can't see the computer keys . . . one more sec . . . okay, okay, I'm better now.

So, let me guess, what really happened was this: You dated a bunch of creeps in college. After seven years of the singles scene, you eloped to Vegas with the pizza delivery guy because you loved each other and you were knocked up. You couldn't fit into Grandma Lilly's wedding dress if you removed your internal organs, so you wore a white maternity dress and your best friend's diamond necklace, because she would have nothing less for you. Your family quit speaking to you because of the pizza guy, and so in front of a justice of the peace, and an Elvis impersonator, you and your husband were married.

Now, exactly 3.3 years later, you're sitting in your cozy two-plus-two duplex in Van Nuys, California, with your potty-training kid who has constant accidents. In fact, she's had more accidents than a crash test dummy. All the while, your husband lies on the couch in the den watching *E! True Hollywood Story* exposés on supermodels, attempting to train the dog to fetch him a six-pack from the fridge. It's crazy, I know. But it's home. And while it's not what you expected, and definitely not what you'd planned, you still find yourself comfortably happy—albeit frustrated and exhausted from living in a place that constantly smells like bodily waste.

The moral to this story is this. The only thing constant in life is the steady stream of laundry that you'll have to do when you try to potty train a toddler. Accidents go with potty training like old people go with Branson, Missouri. Here's the good, the bad, and the poopie that you'll need to know about accidents.

The Anatomy of a Mishap

I guarantee you that the philosopher who said, "There's no such thing as an accident" never had to potty train a toddler. If he did, the expression would have most certainly been, "There are many reasons for an accident." And no truer words would ever have been spoken. For just as there are several methods of potty training, there are several reasons for a mishap. This of course comes as no surprise to any wise mommy, or any professional preschool (which is why having a change of clothes nearby is standard practice). When looking into reasons for an accident, look no further than this list:

Concentration: Nothing is better in parenting life than a child who is so engrossed in an activity that he leaves mommy alone for a long chunk of time. However, this kind of concentration is also fertile ground for an accident. The child is so focused on what he's doing that he totally ignores the signs of a full bladder. Ah well, with every blessing comes a curse, or at least a wet pair of undies.

Excitement: Toddlers are like puppies. Not only will they seek and destroy, but they also piddle when they get overexcited. Of course, this will happen at the most thrilling yet least desirable times: during parades, dance recitals, movies, relay races, and Wiggles concerts. What better time to pee on yourself than while on Mr. Toad's Wild Ride or Splash Mountain. In fact, I have come precariously close to doing the same myself, which is why I stay away from roller coasters and log rides.

Rebellion: This is a biggie. Whether conscious or unconscious, a child might fail to perform in the potty department as a way of showing you who is really the boss. As we all know, in this department it's him.

Stress: Change. It's a four-letter word to most toddlers (mainly because they can't spell worth a damn). A new school, a new babysitter, a new brand of cheese, anything that can cause a child any anxiety can also cause an accident. (This includes parental pressure to potty train.) So if you bring home a new baby sister or even a new cable provider, don't be surprised if Junior brings home a load of poop in his pants.

Holding it in: Just as a kid can be so tired that he can't sleep, he can also be so full of pee that he can't get himself to do it. If a child holds it in too long, his bladder becomes so full that he may lose the sensation of having to pee. If this happens, the simple act of running the faucet should get the river a-flowin'.

Medical issues: A urinary track infection, or any number of medical conditions can make continence difficult. If your child has recurring accidents, is constantly wet or soiled, yet is ready to potty train, consider the possibility that a physical problem might exist and consult your pediatrician.

Unconscious triggers: If you want to get psychoanalytical, I suppose you can reason that some children have accidents as a means of not growing up. I mean, who can blame them. I'd much rather be three years old than forty-three. You can nap every day and eat junk without the worry of getting saddlebags.

Still, the number-one reason for accidents— and I'll bet you know where I'm going with this—is that the child is not yet ready to be potty trained. If you find that your little one is having more accidents than not and does not have

> ❝ I'm a stay-at-home mom and am so desperate for a break, that sometimes I let my son keep building that Lego tower, even though he's doing the pee-pee dance. I know that he's going to have an accident any minute, but I figure, even with the cleanup time ahead of me, I'll still have a longer break than if I stopped him to take him to the bathroom and break his concentration. ❞
>
> —Marla

a medical issue, you might be wise to consider that your timing is off. Unless your child is adamant about continuing with the training process, a return to diapers could be in order. After all, not only are wet or dirty underpants incredibly uncomfortable, they are also embarrassing and can undermine the burgeoning self-esteem of a sensitive toddler. And let's face it, they're a pain in the ass to clean.

Which brings me to the question of what you should do when your trainee has an accident. The answer is not a whole hell of a lot. Keep in mind, it's not your body and you don't have power over it, at least not in this department. But while you can't prevent an accident, there are some things you can do that will make them go down more smoothly for you and your child.

First of all, it's important to realize that with the exception of the rebellious kid who's just a few years shy of having a pack of Marlboros rolled up in his sleeve, kids don't want to have a slip up. Unless you're dealing with a power struggle, your child wants to please you. So when an accident does occur, realize that it's not personal, and that, even though he does it on the one day when you don't bring a change of clothes with you, he didn't do it on purpose.

If your little one has a misstep, it's best to be casual and matter of fact. Let your child know that accidents happen and then maybe even give him a hug, albeit a distant kind of hug that you'd give to someone who just came in contact with a skunk. Then, clean up your child and change his clothes. I find it's best to keep the change of clothes in a large zip-close bag so that you can put the soiled clothes inside of them once they're removed.

Restrain yourself and don't discipline your toddler for having an accident. It will only make matters worse. This is neither the time nor the place for discipline. There will be plenty of opportunities for that later on—like when your kid feeds the goldfish to your dog or uses your new MAC lipstick to practice writing his name on the living room sofa. Not only will scolding, yelling, and punishing reduce your child's self-esteem to zero, it may also cause enough anxiety to assure further accidents, or better yet, provide a launching pad for a battle of wills that you will certainly lose.

Don't get me wrong. If your child has an accident because he was so engrossed with his Leapster that he completely ignored your suggestions to take a potty break, then it's perfectly okay to turn off that freaking little computer until the mess has been cleaned up (if possible, with help from your little one). You can also do the one-two punch of following this up with a casual conversation about what just happened and how to prevent it in the future. You can say the potty-training mantra, "Next time, listen to your body," but those words seem to do as much good as when you program your computer to block that endless stream of penile enhancement e-mail ads.

Plan B

The only thing in the world that is for certain is that nothing is for certain. Parenting is a freeform experience with no predetermined, sure-fire tested set of rules to follow. And when it comes to children you can't plan on anything except the unexpected—especially when dealing with potty-training accidents.

If you've been at it for months and have tried every which way to work it through with your child—supportive, fun, upbeat, patient—and still the accidents keep coming, it's time to reassess the situation. Even if the signs are there, it could be that your child just isn't ready for this developmental milestone. You should consider whether there is a deeper issue at work here. Did you over-nag? Have you reduced your child's self-esteem to a colorless mound of Silly Putty?

It might be wise to hang up the towel for a while, but first you'll want to speak with your pediatrician to make sure there is no physical problem in play. Perhaps even enlist your pediatrician to have a casual conversation about potty training with your child. Sometimes a neutral party is just what the doctor ordered.

If this doesn't help, take a step back and rethink how you want to proceed. Do you stay the course or abandon ship? How much of your life and personal comfort are you willing to give up? Most importantly, how is this affecting your child? For the little one who truly wants to potty train and can't, this can be an especially difficult period, one that will require extra sensitivity and shoring up from you. Assure your child that he will be potty trained at some point soon, it's just going to take a little more time. In the meantime, take my advice and step away from the potty.

More than ever, now is that time to take a little time off, do some research, get some support, and take a much-needed break that involves sandy beaches, exotic drinks, and cute cabana boys. This is not the end of the world—it's toilet training. When you feel stronger and well rested, you can sit down with your child and formulate a new game plan. Do not let your parents, in-laws, neighbors, or the crazy woman at the post office chime in with her opinion on what you should be doing. It is for you and your offspring (and maybe your husband, if he is a Wonder Dad) to decide how you want to proceed and how you want to handle accidents.

Whatever you settle on, when you re-enter the potty-training arena, it should be with a positive attitude. In the end, as with everything with kids, try to make it fun. I know this sounds impossible, but remember—you can do anything. You are woman; hear you roar at your spouse when he cleans your nonstick pans with steel wool. I know you can do it.

Sometimes the best way for you to deal with the reluctant trainee is to do nothing at all. Rather, put your child in charge of his own potty training. Let him choose whether or not he wants to continue and whether he wants to wear diapers, training pants, underpants, or whatever. Then shut up. Be there if and when needed with clean clothes and a good stain remover, and when not, have some of those exotic drinks anyway. And that cute cabana boy, if he happens to be the father of your child. If not, just stick with the drink, because getting involved with a cute cabana boy could get you into more deep doo-doo than you'll ever have with potty training!

Ten Reasons to Love Diapers

If you do decide to put a pause on potty training, don't despair. There are plenty of reasons to love those absorbent, convenient diapers!

1. You never need to use a port-a-potty, most of which smell so vile, they can kill even the worst sinus infection with one good whiff.

2. You don't have to beg a pilot to make an emergency landing because your kid refuses to use a toilet that's filled with blue water.

3. You don't have to deal with cleaning a tightly locked toddler tush.

4. You never have to knock down Santa during the holiday mall rush to get to a toilet—NOW!

5. You don't have to pull into the emergency lane on a road trip so that your kid can pee in the spare potty you keep in the back seat.

6. You don't need to wake Junior from his unexpected and desperately needed nap by spreading plastic wrap between his tush and your new sofa cushion.

7. You don't have to use the pooper scooper to clean up after your kid in the yard.

8. You don't need to be embarrassed standing in line at the bank when your son announces at the top of his lungs that he just farted and the poo-poo is coming now!

9. Dinner at the in-laws is a breeze.

And the saved-the-bet-for-last, most wonderful, fabulous, splendiferous thing about diapers that you will forever appreciate and miss when it's gone is . . .

10. You don't have to deal with public toilets!!!

An Ounce of Prevention
Is Worth a Pound of Poop

As every good Girl Scout knows, it's always good to be prepared. I can think of no other situation where this holds truer than potty training. If you're in the thick of it, you can plan on accidents to happen—at home and on the go. It is your job as the mommy, teacher, and guide (not to mention occasional trashcan whenever your kid has a sticky ice cream wrapper to throw away) to have all the necessary accoutrements on hand at all times.

On the home front, this means paper towels, cleanser (carpet and floor), and possibly a scent absorber such as Carpet Fresh, baking soda, or good ol' Borax. Out in the wide world, you'll want to always have a spare set of clothes, from top to bottom (including shoes and socks), plenty of wipes, and a bag for storing soiled garments. Yes, you'll need to carry a total transformation with you at all times. If you thought that your diaper bag was full when your kid was in Pampers, wait till you see the luggage-size

container that you'll need to cart around now. Forgetting to have these things nearby will ensure
an accident. I cannot begin to fathom why, but it
happens without fail. It's one of the mysteries of
the universe, like your power going out during
the hot scene of *Grey's Anatomy,* and should just
be accepted as a certainty.

Of course, avoiding any or all of these causes
of accidents would also be a wise move:

- If your child is a procrastinator, or prone to
  preoccupation, a placid prod to pee in the
  potty would be prudent.
- If your child wets when excited, avoid
  rocket rides to the moon or frenzied games
  of tickle tackle. If you're faced with such an
  event, try PODS. They're like little femi-
  nine napkins that kids can wear in their
  underpants to absorb small accidents.
- If your child wets when tired and cranky,
  put him to bed.
- If a UTI, constipation, diarrhea, or any
  other technical difficulties are causing
  accidents, take your kid to the doctor.
- Also, avoid anything that can cause a medical malfunction such as bubble baths, perfumed soaps, and psychedelic toilet paper.

- If the pee is stuck in the bladder, run the faucet to help your child "let go," or try a warm bath (for your kid, not you).
- Avoid suspenders, fancy hooks and buttons, padlocks, straightjackets, or any other obstacles to freeing the necessary equipment.
- If your child wants to remain a baby, extol the virtues of being grown up, like staying up late or dirty weekends in Vegas.
- If your child is afraid of public toilets, a portable toilet seat adapter couldn't hurt, or you might even carry the potty chair in your trunk.
- Slow down. If you don't give your child time to go to the potty, your child won't go to the potty. If your child has his BMs exactly ten minutes after he eats breakfast every day, don't shuttle him off to day care five minutes after eating his Cheerios.
- Look for clues to any new stressors at school or at home. Remind the teacher or babysitter to remind your child to go potty.
- Do not withhold fluids. It will not make any difference in wetting mishaps and can be very dangerous.

- Never ever shame, scold, or name call. This will get you a brokenhearted child, no fewer accidents, and costly therapy bills in the future.

While you're at it, don't bother with the whole "You need to go potty before we leave" song and dance until your child is completely potty trained. A two-year-old does not comprehend the notion of "There won't be bathrooms at the drugstore," or "We aren't going to have access to a potty for two hours." Toddlers have no concept of time, and can't produce a pee if they aren't feeling the urge. After all, they are only just beginning to understand what the "urge" is. It is your job, whenever away from home, to have a public restroom in sight at all times, sort of like the way you should locate the exit signs on a plane before takeoff. Because when nature calls on a potty-trainee, it calls loud and it calls fast. And when Junior says, "Mommy, I need to go *now*," you better have a place to go *now* or it's going in the pants. I know that this seems like a lot to remember, and it is. For if potty training is anything, it's a time for mommies to be totally stressed out that they didn't do enough to stop an accident.

With that in mind, know that there are certain situations that promise to produce an accident, such as these:

- Group baths with cousins or playmates.
- A lunch of applesauce and apricots, followed by a movie where a lot of candy is consumed.
- Swims in your neighbor's pool.

Do yourself a favor and stay miles away from the above scenarios during this fragile training period. And if your kid must swim before he's completely, totally, and certifiably potty trained, for the love of Thomas the Train, keep the swim diaper on your kid or you're certain to face your neighbor's water bill after she has to drain her

66 We were invited to a swim party at my boss's house and my kid pooped while I was carrying her in the shallow end. I don't know what came over me, but I scooped up the poop and chucked it in the bushes without anyone being the wiser. It was like I was on the SWAT team and it was a bomb! 99

—Deb

pool because of the lone poop deposited by your three-year-old.

Travel all but guarantees accidents as well. In fact, if you're just about to start potty training, I advise you to delay it until after you get back. Let's face it: A disposable diaper is a traveling mom's best friend. If you must go on the road with your trainee, have a game plan, as well as an itinerary at hand. If you're driving, stay close to your friendly McDonald's. Not only do they have great fries, I've found that they also have really clean bathrooms. Keep a roll of TP in the car so that, in a pinch, your child can pinch off some poop on the side of the road. Yes, it's gross, but it's a whole lot grosser to do it in his car seat. When it comes to potty training, it's all a matter of finding the least gross thing to deal with.

Still, the absolute worst possible habitat for training tots has got to be an airplane. If you must take a family vacation that involves a plane, make sure that you bring along more changes of clothes than fish-shaped crackers, because more than anything in life, you don't want to be stuck 40,000 feet above sea level with a kid who has to use a pillow case for pants. Better yet, leave the kid at home with your in-laws, and go with your hubby for a second honeymoon. The two of you could use it. Just remember to use birth control. I can't imagine anything worse than dealing with potty training *and* morning sickness at the same time.

Remember, you are the one who wants your child potty trained, so you need to do your part. Don't keep your child waiting, and have all the necessities on hand to keep him comfortable and dry. Be proactive; be clear about your expectations; anticipate disaster; and have some of those McDonald's fries from time to time. They really are quite fantastic.

Jump on the Night Train

There you are, all cocky and confident because you finally have Junior in his big-boy underpants. I can see that "My kid is potty trained" smile on your face. But I know your secret. I know that at night you hear a little voice inside that whispers, "Is he really potty trained?" "Can I truly claim victory?" "If I lie still enough, will my husband think I'm sleeping and won't try to have sex tonight?" It's okay, my friend. It's time to get it out in the open and stand up and admit the truth: Your name is Mom, and your kid still wears diapers at night.

No worries. It's perfectly normal, and more common than forgetting to take a plastic bag with you when you walk your dog. Just because your child is potty trained during the day does not mean he's able to stay dry at night. Nor should he be. His brain is still developing, and his plumbing is still maturing. And I can promise you that the fastest way to creating a bed-wetting issue is to take away the Overnights too soon. Interestingly enough, our wee ones can go longer during the dark hours without going wee because the kidneys "go to sleep" right along with our child, ergo producing less urine. Nevertheless, this does not mean Junior can go the distance without a diaper.

Your average, everyday, run-of-the-mill kid generally becomes dry at night somewhere around three years old. Again, boys tend to be later than girls. Research suggests that a delay in night training can also be hereditary. Other factors could be a small bladder, hyperactivity, and the good ol' all-American deep sleeper. On average, studies show that by about age five or six, all but a few kids are ready to have a sleepover without worry.

What you need to know for certain is that there is absolutely no way to train a child to stay dry at night. A child will stay dry through the night when and only when that little bladder is ready to do so—and not one minute sooner. So, unless you like washing sheets, don't even think about taking off those night diapers until you receive some of these following tried-and-true signals:

- Your little one consistently wakes up dry after naps and wakes up in the morning without a wet diaper.
- He can go for several hours during the day without going potty.
- He tells you that he wants to give up his diapers at night.
- He wakes up in the middle of the night to go pee.

If you are confident the time is right, speak with your child about giving it a go, and if Junior gives the idea a thumbs up, go for it. But first, get yourself a waterproof mattress protector and *then* go for it. You can try waterproof sheets, but I find they can smell and feel more like a punishment than an aid. Try putting a plastic pad on top of the mattress, covered by the usual comfy sheet. Make sure to provide a nightlight, and push away all the toys on the floor to create a clear path to the toilet. If the bathroom is miles from Junior's room, you can put the potty chair right there in the room with him (although this could be opening a whole new can of worms).

Be sensitive to the fact that some little tykes find it scary to walk the halls in the middle of the dark, cold night in search of a potty. If this is your tot, make sure you are within earshot of his beckoning call. You can even break out the old infant intercom during this transition phase. And don't throw it away even when you're done. Those things will come in handy years from now when your daughter wants to have boys over to "study."

The great thing about night training is there really isn't much for you to do. Still, there are plenty of things for you to don't:

- Don't restrict drinks. Then again, I wouldn't have your kid chug-a-lug a Big Gulp right before bedtime, either.
- Don't let your child have caffeine or sugary sodas. They will go through your child quicker than a mom through a box of Thin Mints.

- Don't make a big deal of successes or failures. (Remember how well that worked
  when you were day training?)
- Don't scold or punish an accident. Your kid
  was asleep, for God's sake. He didn't want
  to wet the bed. Nobody wants to sleep in
  a puddle of pee.
- Don't be in a hurry. Remember, Mother
  Nature is in charge on this one, and she
  only answers to herself. Sure, we try to
  take charge by doing things like mess-
  ing up the ozone, but she gets us back
  with things like sunspots and premature
  aging.

Most kids, if ready, weather the transition
into night dryness without incident. Some however, are not completely dry until well after their
fifth birthdays. And still more fight bedwetting—technically known as enuresis—for years
to come. If that happens to your child, a private
conversation with your pediatrician might be in
order. There are treatments available, such as nose
sprays or alarms. Your child can also wear special
undergarments that resemble underpants to keep
his bed dry, your laundry basket empty, and your
stress level down.

Regardless, you don't want to make a big deal about night wetting accidents. The bottom line is that these children are not developmentally ready to be dry at night. Until they are, accidents can be a devastating blow to their self-esteem and to your expensive mattress. Other kids don't really care and can sleep on a wet sheet just as easily as a dry one. They'll just wake up in the morning, roll out of bed, and sit down on your couch in their urine-soaked jammies. These are the kids who, when they grow old, will have a much easier time in their facilitated nursing home.

Chapter 6

be careful what you whiz for

Oh, how this whole potty-training ordeal has changed you. You've been in this hell for so long that you've forgotten what it was like to not have poo in your hair, pee on your shoes, and your marriage in shambles. You can't remember how it feels not to be attached at the hip to an angry toddler, whom you resent more than the fact that there will be no *Sex and the City* movie. You have a faint recollection of playing with a beautiful, happy baby; lunching with your friends; and occasionally having sex with your husband, but maybe that was just a dream.

161

Now life as you now know it is a wasteland—
literally. You're a dung beetle on a spinning wheel
caught in a never-ending cycle of chasing down
poo-poo and pees, emptying bowls of excrement
into the toilet, and wiping puddles of stray piss
off various types of flooring. You don't dare invite
people over for fear that they'll comment on your
urine-scented home, step in something just plain
nasty, or find something floating in yet another
unflushed toilet. You're a lonely hermit whose
only companion is your child's goldfish, and
you have to clean up its crap, too! You're spent,
defeated, depressed. You are Mom.

I realize that it's much easier said than done,
but try not to let it get you down. I know just
how you feel. This is not what you signed on for
all those years ago, during your romantic weekend getaway when your child was conceived. Back
in those naïve days, you thought all you'd do if
you had a beautiful baby was stare at her lovingly
all day long. Yes, my friend, the grass is always
greener on the other side, even now that your
grass has turned brown due to your kid's pee.

Not long ago, you were sick of changing dirty
diapers, exhausted from wrestling your kid flat
long enough to change her, and tired of the Desitin stains on your black cardigan sweater. Your

life was filled with poop under your fingernails, stinky diaper pails, and the midnight runs to the grocery store because your good-for-nothing husband forgot to pick up the Pampers on the way home from work yet again.

Sound familiar? After two and a half years and approximately 4,914 diaper changes, you were ready for a kid who went to the bathroom whenever the urge hit and wiped herself so clean that you could see your reflection in her genitals. As any good desperate mommy would do, you decided it was time to potty train your child. But now, six months later, you realize that you might have started training too soon. Junior wasn't ready, even though you certainly were. And so you've faced a thousand more messes without the luxury of containment in a white absorbent square. No, you've had to walk, drag, or carry your screaming child to the bathroom; remove her clothing; cajole, beg, and bribe her to sit on the john; clean up the mess; and then redress the little pisser. And that was if you were lucky! If you didn't make it to the potty in time, it then required a complete change of clothes, cleaning fluid, rubber gloves, and a radiation suit.

But you're a stubborn girl, and rather than throw in the pee-soaked towel, you've decided to stick with it. You're in the throes of it now, and there's no turning back. So you bravely persevere, knowing that it may take yet another thousand attempts before your kid reaches the magic age of three-and-a-half when, in spite all your efforts, she finally does it on her own anyway.

Until that time, there are still a few more challenges you need to know about. A few more tidbits of training you should know before you pull yourself out of the damp and stinky trenches. As they say, knowledge is strength (or is it that there's strength in numbers)? I'm too tired from potty training to remember! All I know is that there are some lessons to learn in this whole excrement arena. So, get out your number two pencils and a bottle of aspirin, and get learning.

Stress

Our dear children are as special and individual as frosted flakes, and that applies to potty training. Each has her own body rhythms, communication skills, timing, and personality, and never do two kids train in exactly the same way. Some sail through the training process with no issues or complications, while others take each and every turn as if they were Mr. Magoo.

A lot of your success in this arena has to do with your child's ability to process change or, more aptly worded, stress. What causes stress for one child may be an unrecognizable event to another. Regardless, a child's stress should be recognized and respected, not demeaned or scolded. Neither temperament is right or wrong, better or worse, richer or poorer. And while I'll grant you that one disposition may be easier to train than the other and is better suited to take with you to a nice restaurant, these are the character differences that make your child a distinct and precious spirit, one who warrants oodles of adorable photos on your fridge.

Because of this, your best bet when trying to potty train is to expect nothing. Be happy for the successes, and be prepared for the setbacks and complications—because you're going to get them by the diaper-pail full! Anything that causes your child anxiety can send her back to a previous stage of development. It's as if she rolled the dice and landed on the "Do Not Pass Go; Do Not Become Potty Trained" square of life.

The most obvious setbacks come with the usual suspects: illness, death, divorce, travel, moving, a new sitter, or the dreaded arrival of a baby brother or sister. If you can see any of these scenarios on the horizon, I encourage you to delay your potty training until the event has passed, as it will most likely delay the learning process. If, however, you find yourself already in the midst of potty training when crisis occurs, or even if your child is long out of diapers, don't be surprised if you face a regression to the Huggies. Your best line of action is to put the diaper back on, reassure your child that she will be a-okay, and forget about potty training until the emotional upset has passed.

A temporary return to diapers is really no big deal in the grand scheme of things. Potty training is like an onion, and once you start pulling back the layers, you're sure to be in tears. Remember, one layer at a time, my friend. I know how upsetting a setback can be and how desperate you are to get back on track. But I guarantee that things will get better in time. Your child will get used to change. She'll grow to like her new house, the new sitter, and even her new baby brother or sister (in about twenty years or so). Like anything else in life, whether it be potty training or waiting around for that twenty years to pass so your firstborn won't try to set fire to her sibling, it just takes patience.

Public Toilets: The Chamber of Horrors
for the Germ-Phobic Mom

Let's face it: We all hate them. Public restrooms
hold many fears for many of us, whether large or
small. For the mommy, it's a world full of germs,
smells, and the deep-seated embarrassment that
comes from making doo-dee in a room full of
other people. For a child, it's all about the sounds,
odd devices, and surprise flushes; the yucky hard
paper (or no paper at all); the automated seat
cover; or worse, the creepy woman with the facial
hair coming out of the stall that you're about to
enter. Airplane toilets are in a class of terror unto
themselves. While public restrooms should be
avoided at almost any cost, when you gotta go,
you gotta go.

Unless you refuse to leave your house for the
next eighteen years, or unless you carry a potty
seat in your car at all times, it's inevitable that at
some point, sometime soon, you and your little
one will be faced with having to use a public restroom. And honestly, even if you do carry around
a toilet in your trunk, I doubt that your ten-year-
old will be willing to plop down on it in a public park. If he does, he's got far greater problems
ahead of him in life than a few toilet germs.

First off, let's allay some of those fears, Mommy—shall we? My pediatrician assures me that since the only body part that touches the toilet seat is the backside of the upper thighs, it is almost impossible to pick up any unwanted illness from it. Organisms that cause sexually transmitted diseases do not survive on toilet seats long enough to do any harm. In addition, my good friend reminds me that urine is sterile and insists that you can even drink it to survive if you're ever lost in the desert—which is why I will neither be having cocktails at her house anytime soon nor joining her on any weekend jaunts to Palm Springs.

Also, contrary to what they told you in your sixth-grade health education class, you cannot get pregnant from a toilet seat, unless of course you have sex on top of it. The delicate "sanitized for your protection" papers that you so carefully place like lace on glass to protect that precious tushie from those meat-eating germs really only serves to mentally protect your imagination from those meat-eating germs. You need worry more about the door handles and faucets in public restrooms than the toilet seat itself. Truth be told, public telephone receivers carry way more germs than public toilets. And let's not even discuss your kitchen sink, which is the germiest part of your house. Still, even if the entire American Medical Association and God himself backed these claims, I'd still be inclined to practice the "holding it in" technique when faced with anything but the restroom at the Ritz.

When it comes to Mommy school of thought, there are two different scenarios when dealing with a public restroom. For those who are not germaphobic, this is the way it works:

1. Open a stall, put your kid on the toilet, let him do his business, wipe, flush, wash, and go about your day.

For those who refuse to shake hands with anyone, for any reason, and insist on bringing their own silverware with them to restaurants, this is how it works:

1. Before putting your child on a public toilet, flush it to make sure anything left from the previous occupant is sent to the monsters and sewer frogs below.

2. Even if the seat appears clean and dry, cover it with a paper seat cover that you keep with you in your purse at all times, along with

other emergency items like Band-Aids, antiseptic spray, and defibrillating paddles.

3. If the bottom of the roll of toilet paper is lingering on the floor, tear off the soiled section, then apply a bottle of Purell to your hands.

4. After your child goes to the bathroom and wipes, have your little one flush the toilet with the handle that you've covered with a piece of toilet paper as a finger shield. Or, if you've managed to teach her this more advanced maneuver, have her stand up and flush the toilet with her foot.

5. Unlock the stall by covering the handle with your shirtsleeve.

6. Washing is obviously key. Not only should you both wash until the top layer of your skin is removed, but your little one must also use a paper towel to cover the faucet while turning it on and off.

7. After the hands are dry, get another piece of paper to cover the door handle with as you exit the bathroom.

8. Replace the bubble wrap around your kid and go about your day.

66 When my daughter was tiny, I'd make her keep her hands on her head at all times when we were in public restrooms. 'Hands on head. Hands on head,' I would say over and over. It prevented her tiny mitts from touching anything except her adorable little head and kept her hands germ free. 99

—Katie

Even more important than how your kid should sit on the public can is that they should never do it alone. It goes without saying that you should always accompany your little one to the public restroom until she reaches the age of twenty-five, has a child of her own, or works in a profession that requires her to carry a loaded firearm. Also, if you are a mommy with a little boy, you must bring him into the women's room with you until he is mature enough to manage on his own in the men's room. And even then, make sure that you stand right outside the door with a baseball bat in hand.

More complicated is the daddy-with-the-little-girl scenario. If this is the case, my most important piece of advice is that your husband must never ask a strange woman to accompany your daughter into the women's room, no matter how uncomfortable he feels. If he does this, one of the moms with the baseball bats will beat him over the head with it. Instead, have him ask whether there are co-ed facilities available. If the ladies room is small, he can make sure it's empty and then go on in. If he must take your daughter to the men's room, ask him to avoid the urinal line and go directly to the stall. That way you'll avoid the inevitable question of, "Mommy, can we make some of those urinal cakes for dessert tonight?"

I know you don't want to hear it, and I hate to admit it, but truth be told, it's probably a good idea to encourage your child to use restrooms away from home as early and as often as possible, from the one at Grandma's house all the way down to one of the worst public bathrooms around, a port-a-potty. You'll instill comfort and confidence in your toddler's toileting skills and (hopefully) head off any fear of foreign toilets that might waylay your next vacation or, worse, preschool in the fall. Learning to use a potty away from home is an important step in your toddler's growing independence and something you will be eternally grateful for the next time you visit Disneyland.

Wine, with Potty Training, Improves with Age

Having your child fully potty trained by two years of age would be incredible. You'd go through the terrible twos without any potty struggles, and you'd save so much money on diapers that you could pay for other necessities like a bike on her birthday, a phone in her room, and a stint in rehab. Early potty training would also mean easier outings, less leaks and messes, and getting rid of your worn-out diaper bag.

But this scenario doesn't happen very often. Most times, parents are freaked out because their child hasn't shown any readiness yet and he's about to grow underarm hair. But fear not. Late development is a common situation that happens with many other milestones. Some kids walk or talk later than others, and it takes some longer to learn to fling their "pasketti" in your face at mealtime. Besides, there are oodles of advantages to potty training an older child.

For one thing, older kids have the helpful advantage of speaking English, or whatever language you speak. You can communicate with them, and, on a good day, you may even be able to reason with them. There's nothing worse than trying to explain basic wiping techniques to someone who can only look at you blankly, point, and say "Dah." Understanding the meaning of what is said is a wonderful advantage to potty training, just as it is with ordering fast food from that those annoying staticky intercoms.

A second advantage to potty training an older child is that she has the ability to become embarrassed. Therefore, when she shows up for her first day at pre-K on that brisk September morning, and all the other kids are lined up in a row at their mini-toilets taking steaming pees in the cool morning air, your kid will be mortified when she has to skulk away with some strange teacher to have her diaper changed. As if!!! This is a definite pre-K don't.

Third, an older child's senses are more highly developed. To the young at heart and young in years, poop is fun and fabulous. It is perfume to the infant nose. But as babies develop, so too do their sensibilities. By the time they're approaching the big o-four, poop smells downright stinky (as do your good-morning kisses, which your kid has no qualms telling you smell like daddy's feet).

Fourth, most older kids can reach the toilet and, more importantly, reach the sink to wash their hands after using the toilet. At the very least, they are able to drag a step stool where needed. They also have longer arms, which enables them to manage the high-wire act of sitting on the toilet and pulling off the toilet paper without losing their balance.

Fifth, they can grasp the concept of what constitutes a reasonable amount of toilet paper for wiping. They have the dexterity to peel off just a few squares, as opposed to unspooling an entire roll as their younger counterparts so enjoy doing.

Sixth, they understand the concept of the "inside voice," as opposed to the "outside voice." When you're in an echo chamber, better known as a public toilet, they can quietly comment on the color of their pee, the shape of their poop (like a pine cone!), and the hair on your "bagina."

Finally, four-year-olds have Game Boys, or other possessions that seem to mean more to them than you do. In a pinch, you have a hostage—more effective than any length of timeout in case they misbehave in the potty arena.

So here's a wink and a nod to all of you laid-back moms, probably with older children, who have greater cares and concerns than your youngest one's bowel movements; who are wise enough to wait and not worry; and who sail through the potty-training process with your more mature toddler in tow—without hardship or heartache.

And on behalf of the mothers still training their geriatric kids to use the potty, I'd like to say one thing to those other moms who got their one-year-olds to crawl into the bathroom, hoist themselves atop the potty, and use it correctly: congratulations, and enjoy. Well, two things. Also know that God will get even with you in about ten years, when your teenager is sporting a butt-crack tattoo and a piercing fetish. Or at least I hope he will because life just can't be that unfair!

Bodily Malfunctions

One would think that once your kid was trained and wearing a steady stream of dry underpants that all the weird potty stuff would become a thing of the past. But nooooooo! The potty party continues. There are plenty of fabulous, fun medical issues that can screw up your potty-training efforts just as effectively as nagging, a new baby sibling, or falling into the potty.

Yes, Virginia, there is a Santa Claus, and you can still get diaper rash even though your kid is fully trained during the day. Your child is a black belt in "holding it in," so her urine becomes more concentrated and as acidic as battery acid. In addition, her heinie skin isn't as tough as it used to be, when it was constantly sitting in diaper pee. Put the two together, and you can get a rash as fast as you can say "Extra-Strength Desitin." The cure, of course, would be for your child to be potty trained at night. Until that fantasy becomes a reality, treat it as you would any other diaper rash. You can also try using specially made night-time diapers that are as absorbent as SpongeBob SquarePants.

If your child is suffering from some sort of intestinal virus that causes loose stools, or from out-and-out diarrhea, try to convince her to put her derriere in diapers until it passes. There's no way that little untrained sphincter is going to be able to keep back the gack. Your child is ill, there's ca-ca everywhere, and you don't need to make her feel any crappier by having her poop in her underpants. (Okay, let's be honest, you don't want her pooping in her underpants.) If she refuses to go back to diapers, it's time to put potties around the house like bowls during a rainstorm when you have a leaky roof. As with anything, an ounce of prevention is worth a pound of diarrhea all over the carpet.

Yeast infections are another medical condition that can put a damper on diaper shedding. Yes, it is possible for your little one to get this grownup-sounding condition. Instead of pregnancy, underwear, or stints in a Jacuzzi, they're most often caused by antibiotics. The symptoms include discharge, itchiness, and painful stinging upon urination. I know that when I had a yeast infection when I was pregnant, I was so itchy that I wanted to go at myself with cutlery, so be sure to call your pediatrician before your child pulls open the utensil drawer. Also, forgo anything that might irritate the fragile vaginal area any further like soaps, perfumed bubble baths, or toilet paper with dyes. Stick with loose-fitting clothes that provide adequate ventilation, white cotton underpants (if any), and soft white toilet paper. In the future, it may be a good idea to give your child yogurt if she's taking a round of antibiotics. That's because antibiotics kill off the good bacteria along with the bad, leaving conditions ripe for yeast to grow. The active cultures in the yogurt replace these good bacteria and therefore prevent this horrible condition.

But the Grand Poobah of medical potty training malfunctions is the urinary tract infection

(UTI), which takes its place high atop the list of potty-training demons. Aptly named, a UTI is an infection of the urinary tract, which includes the urethra, bladder, and kidneys. When germs get into the bladder or kidneys, an infection can develop. This can happen for many reasons: backwards wiping (I told you so!), holding it in, bubble baths, too-tight clothes, or "double dipping" (exploring their anus, then their vagina). Also, some girls have unusually formed urinary passages that make them prone to these infections. If your child has persistent, recurring UTIs, it would serve you well to have her checked by a specialist before any permanent damage is done. Oh, and a talk about the perils of "double dipping" couldn't hurt either.

UTIs most often strike little girls. (When they do occur in boys, it's most often those who have not been circumcised.) They manifest in many ways, ranging from high fever, vomiting, and diarrhea, to having absolutely no symptoms at all. (How many of us pregnant mommies were surprised to discover we had a UTI during a routine visit to our OB/GYN?) Nevertheless, they are fairly common and easily treated. To spot a UTI, look for the following:

- The urgent need to pee, with only a small amount coming out
- Burning and pain while peeing
- Fussiness and lethargy
- Wetting accidents
- Bloody or cloudy urine (which is actually pus in the urine)
- Aches in the mid to lower back

If your child exhibits any of the above symptoms, consider the possibility of a UTI and call your doctor right away. Most likely, she will order a course of antibiotics. As always, you must make sure your child takes all the medicine, exactly as your doctor prescribes (and, as we just learned, a little bit of yogurt wouldn't hurt either). Also, have your sweetie-pie drink lots of fluids so her pee-pee is less concentrated. When fighting a UTI, unsweetened cranberry juice is the fluid of choice for many people, including a lot of old wives, some pediatricians, and, of course, the makers of cranberry juice.

If you child comes down with any of these maladies, it most certainly will put a pause in potty training. But like most other things in life, it's two steps forward and one step back. Take comfort in the fact that when the pain, fever, diarrhea, itching, and burning that accompany these maladies are over, and your kid is back in her itty bitty cotton undies, she will be taking forward steps to the potty once again!

From Potty to Porcelain

It seems like only yesterday that you and your precious Petunia went shopping for that potty chair. She picked out the basic version in her favorite color. You took it home and the two of you decorated it. Then she named it "Benny." From that moment on, Benny became part of the family. He sat with the family around the TV in the evenings. Benny joined you in the kitchen for dinner. He slept in Petunia's bedroom right beside the bed on the floor. He even tagged along on family vacations. He was there for Christmas dinner, the Fourth of July picnic, and your parents' thirty-fifth wedding anniversary. He became more of a companion than the family dog. Yes, if Petunia was there, Benny was not far behind.

And you went along with it—happily. You wanted your child to fall in love with Benny, to feel secure in her toileting attempts. You counted on Benny to get you through this tough

transitional phase. And he did. Benny served
you well—in fact, too well. For now, a year later,
Petunia is completely potty trained, and still
insisting on planting her four-year-old tuckus on
that stinky old poo-stained plastic potty chair. In
fact, she won't potty anywhere except on Benny.
You're sick and tired of it and want Benny to go
far, far, away. *You hate Benny*!

The problem is that in some ways, Petunia
is closer to Benny than to most members of his
own family. Benny has become Petunia's security
object. Forget the binky, blankie, or bunny, Petunia is a big girl now, and she wants Benny. It's not
surprising when you think of all the emotional
wrangles that are tangled up in the potty-training
process. What's a mom to do, short of hiring a hit
man from Jersey (they'll take out anyone for the
right price).

First off, don't panic. This is a very common
conundrum. Even though your kid still likes to
eat sand at the park, she's not as weird as you
think. Secondly, don't stress about it. Although
moving a child from a beloved potty chair to a
big-kid's toilet could be as difficult as getting her
to use the potty in the first place, it *is* possible
with a little finesse and tolerance. If it doesn't
work, the worst thing that can happen is that

Petunia's going to be in for some serious teasing when she hits the college dorm.

You can try waiting it out. Perhaps your child will show an interest in making the transfer on her own (yeah, right!). If, in spite of your serene understanding and patience, you still see no transfer on the horizon, you can try the following:

- Just as you did with Benny, take Petunia with you to buy a toilet-seat adapter. There are dozens of styles in various colors and superhero motifs so that your kid can get just as addicted to this object as well. For travel, pick up one of those toilet seat adapters that folds up like origami.
- Provide a stepstool so that access to the towering toilet is convenient and easy. (It will also serve as a surface for her little feet so they aren't dangling in space when she's seated on the pot.)
- Move the potty chair into the bathroom next to the big toilet so at least your kid gets used to the proximity and environment.

If all else fails, you can try what my friend Maggie did to rid her children of their pacifier and bottle addictions: She had a visit from the Potty-Chair Fairy. Her child placed the potty chair by the front door before bed on the designated night. While she was sleeping, the Potty-Chair Fairy came and took the potty chair away, leaving a brand-new coveted toy in its place.

Sorry, Benny, but once that little gal gets a load of her brand-new princess tiara, you'll be instantaneously forgotten. I know, it's sad. You deserve more for your life of service. You worked hard, took a lot of crap, and never complained. May you lead a fulfilling afterlife being recycled into dozens of plastic spoons.

My Toilet Runneth Over

There is one side effect to potty training that I bet you were never warned about. It really should come as no surprise, considering the massive amounts of poop you've already found inside your child's diaper. But since it was often all smushed up like a stinky wad of frosting, it was difficult for you to make out its original shape. Had you been able to, you could have predicted that a side effect of poop training would have to be the clogged toilet.

You'd think that with those tiny little bodies, those tiny little digestive systems, and those teeny-tiny little colons, that poops would be bitty little things. *No*. This miniature person who once fit inside of your uterus can produce a poop just as big as she was when she emerged from your body. In fact, toddler's poops can often be so large that after they go to the bathroom, their waistbands are actually loose! Therefore, once your child is trained to poop in the potty, you, as the person in charge of this mini poop factory, will indeed find yourself faced with a clogged toilet. When this happens, you have several options to choose from:

Call a plumber: Sounds like a good idea, but a plumber can be expensive, and he will most definitely *not* believe that your little three-year-old made the massive dump now clogging your commode. He will nod his head, chuckle, and give you a facetious smile that says, "Yeah right. Your kid did it." He'll spend two minutes in your bathroom, unclog the toilet, hand you a bill for $150, then laugh all the way to his truck as you yell after him, swearing up and down that it wasn't you.

Shut the door to the bathroom until your husband gets home from work: This idea only works if you have more than one bathroom and your husband is handy around the house. Even then, you still have to convince another adult that you are not the culprit. What's worse is that he lives with you, so you will be hearing about it for the rest of your life. At parties, family gatherings, business soirees, just put one drink in him and out he'll come with the story of your massive dump of '07, the one that clogged the toilet to Kingdom Come.

Call your mom and dad: Nah, this quit working when you left for college.

Have your nanny or housekeeper unclog the toilet: This only works if you have a nanny or housekeeper, and even then, there is no Christmas bonus large enough to compensate for such a chore.

Do it yourself: Yes, sister, I'm afraid it's true. After exhausting all possible alternatives, your only real option when your kid clogs the toilet is to get down and dirty and unclog the darn thing yourself. Don't worry. In a weird way, mastering the technique of clearing a toilet can be an empowering experience for a woman. If not, at the very least you will know what to do if and when you do clog it up yourself. Just follow these

few simple steps, and your pipes will be a-flowin'
lickety split:

1. Put the perpetrator, a.k.a. your child, in a safe
   spot where she will be contained and occu-
   pied for several minutes (i.e., strapped into
   her stroller in front of the TV). You don't
   want her to watch you do this or she might
   try it herself. Also, for the neophyte toilet
   trainee, a clogged toilet can be a scary thing.
2. If the water is running, causing a continuous overflow, shut off the valve located on
   the underside of your toilet. If you can't
   find it, or if it's shut so tight that you can't
   get it to turn, then you'll need to shut off
   the main water line. In most cases, this is
   in front of your house. Make sure you know
   where your water shutoff valve is before you
   begin potty training.
3. If the plugged water is still, do not be
   tempted to flush again and hope for the
   best. This will cause all that poopie water
   to pour out onto your bathroom floor. Your
   toilet's exit pipe is blocked. Flushing will
   just cause more water to go into the bowl,
   without allowing any to flow out.

4. Take your handy-dandy plunger and place the suction end over the exit hole at the bottom of your toilet bowl. This is gross, I know, but it's the only way. You must make sure that the plunger forms a continuous seal around the hole or you will not be able to create the force needed to blow that poop from the pipe.

5. Plunge. Push in and out on the wooden stick attached to the plunger head so that force builds inside the pipe. This is where everyone asserts his or her individuality and style. Some people prefer fast and frantic plunges. Others like slow methodical plunges. Some use a combination of the two. I could make an analogy to sex here, but I'm fairly grossed out as it is.

6. As you do this, the water level of your toilet bowl will gradually sink. This is good. It means the water, and the clog, are slowly but surely being pushed down into the sewer system with the sharks, snakes, and crocs.

7. If you've turned off your water line, you can try turning it on again.

8. When the water is almost completely drained from the toilet, go for a flush. The

water will rise and hopefully settle back down again.

9. You might need to plunge many times before the toilet flushes freely and unencumbered.

10. Afterwards, place the dirty plunger in your fireplace and burn it. If you don't want to do this, if for some reason you feel you must salvage this heroic instrument, pour some chlorine bleach over it, put it in the middle of your back yard, and give it a good hosing off before allowing it in the house again.

11. Wash your hands. Better yet, take a hot bath. You deserve one.

You want to make sure that you have a plunger for every bathroom. There's nothing worse than watching that brown water rise and having no idea where the heck your plunger is. Also, please don't use your bathroom plunger in your kitchen sink, otherwise your entire family could end up with an intestinal funk that's sure to clog your toilets, if not put you in the hospital.

Now would be a good time to explain the mid-poop flush to your child, especially if he's prone to clogs. You will also need to reinforce the importance of using a reasonable amount of toilet paper when wiping. This type of "pity flush" is key if a lot of wipes are in order. After all, when it comes to clogged toilets, prevention is truly the way to go.

Till Death Doo-Doo You Part

One of the least discussed side effects of potty training is how stressful it can be on your relationship with your significant other. As with other aspects of child-rearing, like nighttime feedings and tantrums, dealing with them can be more upsetting than forgetting to set your TIVO for the season finale of Dancing with the Stars. Sure, there are those few experiences that can bring you closer together. At times, you'll catch a glimpse of your child and husband playing together, and you'll see a side of him that'll amaze you and make you fall more deeply in love than you ever thought possible. Unfortunately, potty training is not one of those experiences.

In fact, potty training has some sort of supernatural component that magically seems to make men disappear altogether. As soon as the potty-training experience begins, they vanish. *Poof*! Then, *poof*! They magically reappear just as suddenly when the potty-training process is complete. I don't know exactly where they go, but I imagine they're all together on some tropical desert island enjoying fine Scotch, Cuban cigars, and discussing lawn care. All the while, we women slog through the wet and stinky trenches back home. You'll see. As soon as your kid is finally potty trained, your man will suddenly reappear with just the hint of a tan and a new power edger.

I know it's not fair, yet we must accept it as just another one of the inequities between the sexes, like the ability to have a sex drive at any given point on any given day. But I promise you this. I'm going to find that desert island, and I will personally throttle each and every one of those daddies before hurling them into the big blue and claiming that island for myself, my mommy friends, and the entire DVD collection of *Sex and the City*—including the last episode with the alternate endings. Ahhh, I can taste the mai tais already. Of course, you're invited too!

The bottom line is that potty training, like any other aspect of child-rearing, can put a strain on your marriage. While I know that Wonder Dads do exist, the brunt of potty training does fall on us mommies. Fine, we can deal with it.

We deal with housework and planning vacations and buying the holiday and birthday gifts for all the members of the family, even when we only have the one sister and he has more siblings than a litter of puppies. We do these things because what choice do we have? Besides, sometimes it's easier to do it ourselves. Can you imagine what would happen if your mate dared to have a different opinion on how to go about potty training? Or even worse, if his mother had an opinion? And—in by far the worst-case scenario—your husband agreed with his mother? That would truly be a recipe for disaster.

Do yourself a favor. Decide together and ahead of time on your potty-training game plan, be it the long, lingering, gradual approach, or the fast-and-furious intensive one. Should you go with the Dr. Phil method (page 55), or would you prefer the German-grandmother style (page 63)? Even if you're in the middle of the battle already, call for a strategy session. Get all those opinions out and on the table. What do you want to do? What does he want to do? If you have to do the heavy lifting, maybe he can do the demonstrations or read the cute and entertaining "potty books" to Junior at night. (To me, that's worth 100 dirty diaper changes right there, as I've grown to hate both Prudence and Joshua more than I hate to fold fitted sheets.)

Once you and your man have a game plan, don't share it with anyone, especially other potty-training parents. They will only make you feel bad and do their best to convince you that their way is better. It's human nature. A seed of doubt will be planted in your brains, and it will grow into a full-blown redwood of anxiety and blame. It's survival of the fittest. The only way one set of parents can feel good about their potty-training method is to take other parents down. If you're bearing the brunt of the training challenge and you're tired of the various remarks from friends, sitters, and Grandma, take it out on your husband. Again, human nature. After all, the reason God invented marriage in the first place was to give moms someone to be pissed off at while potty training their children.

No matter who participates in the potty-training process, for the sake of your child (who, let's face it, is the one that's really in the oven right now), keep the potty training consistent. That last thing that your little tater tot needs is different ways to do his doo-ty. This is the quickest way to get a confused toddler in soiled underwear and a household full of arguing adults.

Certain aspects should go without saying, although when dealing with men, they should probably be said anyway. It's generally easier for Mommy to teach darling daughter about sitting on the toilet to go pee and Daddy to teach Sport how to pee standing up. I mean, really, what do we women know about jiggle drops? It's one of those things that require demonstration. Nevertheless, if you are a single mom, or the wife of a man on the desert island of dads, have no fear. Your little one will be exposed to plenty of jiggling penises in the near future, at preschool, day care, a friend's house, and in life in general. He's sure to pick up this skill along with other important things like the classic playground taunts and the all-important "underarm fart." In the meantime, just keep some Lysol wipes on hand for cleanups.

The bottom line is not to let potty training destroy your relationship. There are far better ways to end a marriage—maybe a gambling addiction or Antonio, the UPS man. Don't throw in the towel over diapers. If your love life is going down the toilet over potty training your child, then perhaps you shouldn't be potty training right now. If it's this difficult, and causing this much strife, chances are Junior isn't ready.

" I've tried a thousand times to describe the tap-tap-tap technique to my four-year-old son, but to no avail. I even tried using my giant hand on that itty-bitty penis to actually show him what to do. But this only got us either a massive case of the giggles, or a deafness-inflicting scream because my hands were so cold. **"**

—Gina

Do yourself a favor and take a break. Put the diapers back on (your child), put a sexy dress on (you), and go out for a hot date (no, not with Antonio!). Try to remember what it was like before the madness. This is the man you *love*, remember. For richer or poorer. In sickness and in health. In Huggies or Pampers. And in the years to come, when your child has grown, and your life has mellowed, you and your man can finally take that romantic vacation to that tropical island that you've always dreamt of. And when you see that gaggle of guys with the scotches and Cuban cigars, throw some sand in their faces and tell them to go home to their wives!

Chapter 7

congratulations!

Hooray! You did it! Your child has finally grasped the difficult feat of urinating and defecating in a socially acceptable way. Not too long ago, when you were knee-deep in doo-dee, you were convinced that this day would never come. But it has, it has! Now, not only does your little spring roll pee and poop in the toilet on a consistent basis, he also wipes himself clean, flushes without clogging the toilet with a roll full of paper, and on a really good day, even remembers to wash his hands without being told . . . with soap no less! He stays dry at night and can even pee on an airplane, the white-knuckler of toilets! Woo hoo! And you were sure you'd be the only parent whose teenager had to wear pull-ups underneath his graduation gown!

At last, you can finally get rid of all the diaper and potty equipment and call your house a home again, instead of just a litter box with crown molding. You don't have to struggle to make anymore "diaper sausages" in your Diaper Genie or scrub your hands more than a surgeon after cleaning up a really messy poop. You can give your old changing table to your next-door neighbor, who just had her first child and thus has years of diaper doo-dee ahead of her. You can finally toss your stash of emergency diapers that you kept on a high shelf just in case of setbacks and can even start to grow your fingernails long once again!

Hip, hip, hooray! You have passed the test and are finally in the club of the other successful moms who have weathered the storm and come through feeling much cleaner and drier. Now, no matter how bad your day was or what other crisis you needed to face, at least you have the power to put it in all in perspective. Who cares if the dog just ate your new sofa and they repossessed the car? At least your kid is potty trained! And now that this venture is behind you and your kid's behind is as shiny as a new penny, you can say it loud and say it proud: "My child is potty trained!" You can finally have that lobster dinner, and enjoy your moment in the sun. But savor the moment because it won't be long before you face your next child-rearing milestone. For if your local public elementary school is overcrowded and underfunded (and whose isn't), then you have to figure out a way to get your kid in an affordable private school that has an opening. And that, my friend, can make potty training seem like a day at the spa.

But until that time, bask in the glory. You've earned it!

Things You Can Do with Your Old Diaper Bag

1. Use it to hide receipts from your husband for things like your overpriced shoes and sofa pillows that you told him were a gift from your sister. He'll never find them in the diaper bag since he refused to touch it even when your kid was in diapers.

2. Have a bonfire and burn it up along with other things you'll never need again, like the shirts you had to wear braless and the old alarm clock that you'll never need again now that you wake up naturally at the crack of dawn anyway.

3. Use it as an overnight bag for all of your romantic getaway weekends with your husband (yeah, right!)

4. Give it to your daughter to use as a bed for her dollies (okay, if your son has dollies, you can let him use it, too).

5. Toss the bag but keep the plastic changing pad. It's a great protective barrier to use between your dining room table and the watercolor masterpiece that your kid is painting.

6. Bring it to the organic market so you won't have to ask for a paper or plastic bag, which are both hard on the environment and often get you a stare from the checkout person.

7. Hang it behind the front seat of your car to store back-seat trash and keep emergency items like Kleenex and carsick bags.

8. Keep it. It's cute and from the Gap, and besides, you can fit a lot of stuff in it. And now that it's not used to lug around soiled clothing, it smells a lot nicer, too!

Appendix

resources section

Hand Washing Songs

Have your child sing the following songs while washing her hands in order to gauge the length of the wash time. If hands are moderately dirty, sing them in an up-tempo beat. If they're really dirty, or you're in a public restroom, you'll want to slow down the tempo a bit.

- "Row, Row, Row Your Boat"
- "Twinkle Twinkle Little Star" (you can change the words to "Tinkle Tinkle" if you want to have some giggles)
- The alphabet song
- "Happy Birthday to You" (but don't record it or it will cost you a ton in royalties)
- Barney's "I Love You" (and then accept that it will be forever stuck in your mind)

A Poem

I saw this one on the door of a public restroom stall, next to the phone numbers of a couple of people I should call for a good time. It's a keeper.

If you sprinkle
When you tinkle
Be a sweetie
And wipe the seatie.

Books to Poop By

It's a sad truth, but children's potty-training books are probably the most boring books on the face of the earth. What's worse, because of all the taboo references to bottoms, pee, poops, and private parts, your child will be titillated to a frenzied state of excitement not yet known. Therefore, he will want you to read them over and over and over again.

Do yourself a favor. As soon as your child goes potty on the pot, accidentally "forget" these books in the supermarket cart.

- *Everyone Poops*, by Taro Comi and Amanda Mayer Stinchecum
- *Once Upon a Potty*, by Alona Frankle (with versions for both girls and boys, illustrations complete with anatomically correct body parts—well, they don't really look all that anatomical, but your kid'll get the gist)
- *The Gas We Pass: The Story of Farts*, by Shinta Cho and Amanda Mayer Stinchecum. This one will make your kid laugh so hard he'll fall off the pot! I know it's not technically a potty-training book, but it's worth it just to see your kid fall off laughing.

Books to Read While Sitting with Your Kid in the Bathroom

If you can take a break from reading to your kid, read a book of your own. But try to make it a book about people going through a more difficult time than you are. Potty training is horrendous, but some of these scenarios may help put your life in proper perspective:

- *The Diary of Anne Frank*, by Anne Frank
- *Middlesex: A Novel*, by Jeffrey Eugenides

- *Tuesdays with Morrie*, by Mitch Albom (inspirational, but also with a focus on the tragedy of Morrie's life)
- Any biography about Princess Di that focuses on her marriage to Prince Charles

Potty-Training Videos

I find that videos can be even worse than the books, since they contain songs that stick in your brain like a benign tumor. But here are some of the most popular:

- *Once Upon a Potty*, by Alona Frankle (also in girl and boy versions)
- *Potty Power for Boys and Girls*, by Potty Power
- *Bear in the Big Blue House: Potty Time with Bear*, by Noel McNeal, Peter Linz, Vicki Eibner, and James J. Kroupa. This video is the best of the worst, with catchy songs and funny sketches. It was obviously produced by sympathetic adults who knew that Mommy and Daddy would be sitting through it a zillion times.

Potty-Training Gadgets

These are available at most baby stores, like Babies 'R Us or the discount stores. You can also let your fingers do the walking and order them on the various potty-supply Internet sites, including *www.pottytrainingsolutions.com*.

- Potty chairs.
- PODS (toddler-sized absorbent napkins used for small accidents).
- Stickers and sticker books (for decorating the potty and as a reward for using it correctly).
- Dolls that pee: Used in the Dr. Phil method of training, or just to have to help your child make the connection of drinking and peeing. I suggest that you only use these in the bathtub. You have enough accidents to clean up, thank you very much!
- Musical potty seats: These are the fad of the moment. Time will tell on this one.
- Johnny light: This device lights up the toilet seat so that your kid can find it in the middle of the night.

- TP Saver: A toilet paper roll lock so that kids can't unroll the whole roll to the floor.
- Clean Care Flushable Wipes Holder: It attaches to toilet paper roll holder so that the wet and dry wipes are housed together.
- Potty on the Go: A traveling potty chair with easy to remove plastic inserts so you don't have to clean out the chair itself.
- Piddling Toilet Targets: If you don't have Cheerios, these colorful flushable targets make for a good aiming target.
- Potty Toppers: These are soft, oversized, disposable toilet seat covers that you can use in public bathrooms.

My Favorite Cleaning Products for Potty Training

The shelves at my house are lined with all kinds of cleaning products, including these:

Clorox disinfectant wipes: Have one handy in each bathroom to clean up messes from the sinks to the toilets to the floors. Sold at supermarkets and discount stores.

Totally Toddler Stain Remover: It's nontoxic and good for removing stains from clothing and sheets. Sold at *www.pottytrainingsolutions.com*.

Bi-O-Kleen Bac-Out Stain and Odor Eliminator with Spray: Naturally gets rid of stains and odors. Sold at Amazon.com.

Begley's Best: This is a line of cleaning products by actor and environmentalist Ed Begley Jr. They work great and are Mother Nature approved. Sold at *www.begleysbest.com*.

Relaxation Techniques

- Deep breathing
- Massage
- Meditation
- Yoga
- Sleep
- Sex
- A fifth of tequila

How to Cook that Celebratory Lobster Dinner

1. Go to the seafood counter and get some precooked lobster tails that have been split in half lengthwise. I know there are people who can just boil a large pot of water and stick a live creature inside, but we're mommies now and this goes against everything that we're about.

2. Rub some softened butter on top of the lobster meat and sprinkle on a few drops of good olive oil. Add a touch of salt and some minced garlic to taste.

3. Melt butter to put in a side dish for dipping.

4. Pop the lobster under the broiler. Cook until the butter gets all bubbly.

5. Enjoy!

index

Accidents, 135–60
    ease of, pee vs. poop, 74–75
    introduction to, 135–38
    at night, 155–60
    pediatrician advice on, 145
    physical problems and, 145
    praising child for reporting, 74
    preparing for/preventing, 149–55
    reasons for, 139–42
    responding to, 142–44, 159, 160
    while traveling, 154–55
Babysitter, training by, 65–66
Bagina, 33
Bed, protecting, 157–58
Bedwetting, 156, 159–60
Beginning training, 7–11. See also Timing, of training
    average age for, 8
    avoiding premature start, 8
    ready for, signs, 9–11
    right time of year to, 11–14
    starting over, 146–47
    stepping back/reassessing, 145–46
    when cold outside, 13–14
    when kids are older, 173–76
    when things are settled, 11–12

Blood, in stools, 118
Books (resources), 202–4
Bottom, words for, 35
Bowel movements. See Pooping
Boys peeing, 76–81. See also Pee, holding in
    "aim and shoot" game, 78–79
    flushing after, 87–89
    jiggle drops, 79–80
    making fountain, 77
    potty manners, 80–81
    proclivities, 94–97
    sitting or standing, 25–26, 77–78
Boys pooping
    girls vs., 107–8
    special challenges of, 107
Cheerios bullseyes, 78–79
Cleaning products, 206–7
Clogged toilets, 184–90
Constipation, 112, 116–22
    causes of, 117–18, 119–20
    causing fecal leaks, 117–18
    diet and, 120–22
    emotions/control and, 114–15
    pain from, 117–18
    rectal fissures from, 118
    signs of, 119
    treating, 120–22
    while traveling, 113

Control
  avoiding issues with, 115–16
  child having, over you, 19–20
  by holding it in, 91–93,
    114–16
Defining potty training, 16–18
Diaper bag, uses for, 199–200
Diapers. *See also* Training pants
  disposable, 9–10, 54–55, 154
  at night, 155–56, 157
  reasons to love, 147–49
  temporary return to, 166
Diarrhea, 118, 150, 177, 179,
  181
"Do nothing" method, 68–70
Dos and don'ts, 21–23
Dr. Phil method, 55–56
Encopresis, 118
Expectations, releasing, 18, 165
Fantasy-world training, 40–43
Fear (child's)
  of change, 11
  of peeing, 86–89, 95–97
  of pooping, 111–13
Fear of success (parent's), 20–21
Flushing
  noise/fear of, 87–88
  teaching, 88–89
Girls peeing, 81–85. *See also* Pee,
  holding in
  in big toilet, 83–84
  ease of, 81
  flushing after, 87–89
  proclivities, 94–97
  standing up, 84
  toilet paper amount, 82

  wiping after, 81–83, 126–27
Gluteus maximus, words for, 35
Goal, of training, 38
Grandmother, training by,
  63–65
Husband, training by, 61–63.
  See also Relationships, potty
  training and
Hygiene
  public toilets and, 167–72
  tips, 131–34
Incentives
  appropriate to your child,
    46–47
  bribes vs., 45–46
  candy as, 47–48
  children tricking you for, 100
  defined, 44–45
  downside of, 48
Infancy potty training, 49–53
Intelligence of toddlers, 100–
  101
Laziness, holding it in and,
  90–91
Length, of training, 14–18
"Make someone else do it"
  method, 60–68
Marriage, potty training and,
  190–95
Medical issues, 176–81
Methods
  "do nothing," 68–70
  Dr. Phil, 55–56
  fantasy world, 40–43
  infancy potty training, 49–53
  keeping your selection

private, 39–40
"make someone else do it,"
60–68
real-world, 43–44
Motherhood
reality of, 5
yearning for, 3–4
Nanny, training by, 65–66
Nighttime, 155–60
Outdoor training, 12–13
Pain
while pooping, 112, 117–18
while urinating, 89–90. *See
also* Urinary tract infection
(UTI)
Paraphernalia, 24–31. *See also*
Potty chair; Toilet
getting rid of, after using,
198, 199–200
Internet site for, 205–6
other stuff, 30–31
training pants, 27–30
Pass gas, words for, 34
Patience. *See also* Reactions
(parent's)
amidst frustration, 18–19,
161–64
getting them to go, 100
not getting pissed off,
97–103
Pee, holding in, 85–93
controlling you by, 91–93
"diaper rash" from, 176–77
fear causing, 86–89
laziness causing, 90–91
pain causing, 89–90

reasons for, 86–93
universality of, 85–86
Peeing, 71–103
away from home, 95–97
boys. *See* Boys peeing
fear of, 86–89, 95–97
flushing after, 87–89
girls. *See* Girls peeing
at night, 155–60
overview, 71–72
responding to urge, 74–75
timing of, 73
urge, connecting, 72–75
words for, 34
Penis, words for, 32, 33–34, 35
Phil, Dr., method, 55–56
Plan, for training, 192–93.
See also Beginning training;
Methods; Timing, of training
Poop
playing with, 128–29
smelly, reacting to, 106–7
wiping effectively, 81
Poop, holding in, 108–16
attachment/possessiveness
causing, 110–11. *See also*
Constipation
controlling you by, 114–16
fear causing, 111–13
reasons for, 110–16
stress as cause, 113
Pooping, 105–34
general challenges of, 106–7
hygiene and, 131–34
idiosyncrasies, 128
kids demanding diaper for,

129–31
overview, 105–8
pain from, 112
timing of training vs. peeing,
   105–6
urge, 105–6
words for, 34
Potty chair
   features of, 24–25
   pros/cons, 26
   toilet vs., 24–27
   transitioning out of, 181–84
Potty training
   defining, 16–18
   dos and don'ts, 21–23
   length of, 14–18
   medical issues affecting,
      176–81
   other names for, 37–38
   outdoors, 12–13
   perspective on, 5–7
   pressures of, 6–7
   relationships and, 190–95
   resources, 201–7
   successful completion of,
      197–200
Potty Zone, 2–3
Privacy, of method used, 39–40
Proclivities, 93–97
Public toilets, 167–72
Punishment, 42, 44, 58, 102,
   159
Reactions (parent's), 97–103
   to accidents, 142–44, 159,
      160
   end of rope, 129–31

expressing/controlling
   emotions, 19, 97–103
fear, 20–21
keeping perspective, 18, 103,
   161–63
to manipulation, 100–101
patience amidst frustration,
   18–19
to smelly poop, 106–7
trusting it will work out, 20
to ups and downs, 99
Zen perspective, 18
Ready for training, signs, 9–11
Real-world training, 43–44
Relationships, potty training
   and, 190–95
Relaxation techniques, 207
Resources, 201–7
Season, to begin training, 12–14
Siblings, training by, 66–67
Sleeping, peeing and, 155–60
Stool, words for, 34. *See also* Poop
Stress
   affecting BMs, 113
   causing accidents, 140, 151
   setbacks from, 165–66
Terminology, of potty training,
   31–35
Timing, of training. *See also*
   Beginning training
   duration, 14–18
   pooping vs. peeing, 105–6
   then vs. now, 53–55
   when it's off, 141–42
Toilet
   accessories for, 25–26